CONTENTS

PART 4 GAINING GREATER INSIGHT INTO YOURSELF AND OTHERS

PART 5 APPENDICES

ACKNOWLEDGEMENTS

There are several people who I would like to thank. This is in no order of merit.

My parents, for having taught me right from wrong, and everything else they did for me (whether I appreciated it at the time or not!).

Lisa Wake, my friend and fellow traveller on life's journey, for her love, support and encouragement, and invaluable guidance whilst writing *Successful NLP*.

All the founders and subsequent developers of NLP.

The many people who have taught me NLP, especially Ian McDermott, Tad James, David Shephard, Robert Dilts, Suzi Smith, Shelle Rose Charvet, John Grinder, Dr Wyatt Woodsmall, Lorraine Flores and Jane Battenberg (apologies for any omissions).

My students and clients, whose willingness to learn and develop is an inspiration to me.

Gabriella Goddard, who planted the seeds of me being an author.

My colleagues Julie, Dave and Henrietta, who have looked after my business while I wrote *Successful NLP*.

Authors of the books referred to in *Successful NLP*.

Ros Edwards, for her friendship and advice.

Allison Harper, for recommending to her colleagues at Crimson Publishing that I write *Successful NLP*.

Lucy McLoughlin, Sally Rawlings, Holly Ivins and Caroline Maddison, at Crimson Publishing, for their patience and encouragement.

FOREWORD

I first came across NLP in the early 1990s as a manager in the NHS. I was seeking a tool kit that would enable me to enhance my communication with others and discovered that many of the tools and techniques of NLP provided useful solutions to everyday communication problems.

Jeremy has encapsulated some of these tools and techniques within this book. He has created a 'must-have' manual for individuals to dip into this skill set. Readers will quickly learn how to use the skills in a practical, effective and safe manner with themselves.

This no-nonsense, practical and readily accessible book provides a perfect introduction for those wanting to find out more about NLP. The book also provides an ideal stepping stone for those who want to find out more before attending a course in NLP.

Lisa Wake
MD Awaken Consulting & Training Services Ltd
Former Chair of UK Council for Psychotherapy
Author of *Neurolinguistic Psychotherapy: A Postmodern Perspective*

INTRODUCTION

Welcome to *Successful NLP*. This book has been written for people like you, people who are interested in discovering just how useful NLP is, and how it can help them to get better results, faster, in all areas of their life. It is written particularly for people who have had either little or no previous exposure to NLP, or those who may have attended a brief course and want to delve a little more deeply.

NLP was initially developed in the mid 1970s, and for a while was treated with some scepticism in certain quarters. It has developed to such an extent that it is increasingly being recognised and accepted academically. For example, there are Masters Degrees in NLP and related topics from a UK university, with a few high-quality NLP courses qualifying for credits towards postgraduate NLP qualifications.

In addition, in 2008 the University of Surrey ran the first International NLP Research Conference, where delegates presented research papers which prove the effectiveness of NLP. Further similar conferences have been planned, and the volume of academically-based evidence that NLP is effective is increasing rapidly.

The purpose of *Successful NLP* is to provide you with information about NLP and how to use it to improve the results you get in life, and to help you to have more of what you want and less of what you don't want.

Successful NLP contains only the minimum background theory, which means it has the maximum amount of information possible dedicated to providing you with useful, practical tips on how to use NLP most effectively.

How this book is structured

The book is divided into four main parts:

Part 1 provides an essential background to the work we will cover in subsequent parts. There is some theory in Part 1 to provide a foundation for the rest of the book.

Part 2 considers communication, the sometimes hidden or subtle meaning of words, and how to use words even more effectively to enhance your communication. It also considers non-verbal communication, which, as you will see, can be even more important than verbal communication.

Part 3 is the bulk of the book, and considers how to change behaviours and responses and hence your results, the 'nuts and bolts' of NLP. For each topic, you will learn why it is useful, the relevant information about the topic and how to use it.

Part 4 covers gaining even greater insight into yourself and others plus a summary of how to apply the information contained in this book.

Finally, the appendices contain a brief word on some of the NLP topics not covered in this book, a summary of how to apply the information written in this book, information about NLP training courses, a references and further reading guide and a glossary of terms.

All of the chapters have exercises, tips and examples of how the techniques have been used with people in all areas of life – business/work, relationships, coaching, sport education and health. Please note that the names (and sometimes the gender) of the people referred to in the examples have been changed in order to preserve client confidentiality.

By the very nature of this topic, some of the techniques will be explained in some detail to enable you to be able to know how to use them.

How to get the most from *Successful NLP*

As mentioned earlier, *Successful NLP* is very much a 'how to' book. There are numerous exercises and, in order to assist you in developing the skill to use the techniques effectively for yourself, the processes are explained step by step. It may be useful, and even necessary, to re-read some of the processes, or refer to them whilst doing the exercises. When I was learning NLP I found that the more I read through and then practised a particular NLP process the better I was able to do it.

It is recommended that you do as many of the exercises as possible, especially those which may initially seem a little challenging to you and which you may find would benefit you. You may want to re-visit sections of this book every few months to refresh your memory – I guarantee that every time you refer to the book you will learn something new because your base knowledge will have increased and therefore you will be reading it through 'new eyes'.

To assist you in working through this book, there is a glossary with an explanation of the main terminology used in this book.

A quick word of caution

NLP coaching techniques are potentially powerful tools and are only to be used in a way that is beneficial to all people involved. They are not to be abused or misused. Although many of the techniques in NLP can be used by qualified NLP Practitioners, Master Practitioners and Trainers to assist others to make changes to various aspects of their life, *Successful NLP* is written primarily for people to use in their own lives. I would strongly suggest that unless you are qualified in NLP, you limit any use of the NLP change techniques (particularly those in Part 3) to yourself.

Although NLP techniques are increasingly being used by medical professionals, therapists and counsellors, they are not a substitute for medical advice, therapy or counselling if that is what someone needs.

And finally...

I hope that you enjoy and benefit from reading the book and using the techniques as much as I have enjoyed and benefitted from learning and using the skills.

PART 1

THE BUILDING BLOCKS FOR SUCCESS

PART 1

CHAPTER 1

What is NLP?

In this chapter, we will cover the basics of NLP so that you can begin to get to grips with the techniques and how to use them. In particular, we will cover:

- What is NLP?
- Some background and history of NLP
- The three main benefits of NLP, and hence why it is so useful
- Some of the main uses of NLP
- What it is and what it is *not*

WHAT EXACTLY IS NLP?

What is NLP (Neuro Linguistic Programming)? There are several ways of describing it.

There are some clues about it in the name. *Neuro Linguistic* is about the language of the mind ie pictures, sounds, feelings, tastes, smells and self-talk. *Programming* relates to the patterns of thinking and behaviour which we all have, rather like computer programs. For example, if someone is asked to make a presentation or speak in public and they are not used to doing this, they may have a nervous response, which is a pattern of behaviour they run. NLP is a series of 'techniques', communication tools, approaches and attitudes to help people to change their patterns of behaviour and communication, so they can have more of what they want and less of what they don't want, and hence achieve their goals.

Another definition of NLP is 'the study of subjective human experience'. Why is it that you will respond in a particular way to an event, and someone else will respond differently? And how can you change your responses if they do not serve you?

Some people simply call NLP 'the new science of success', a way to get better results, faster.

NLP is rapidly becoming seen as a set of tools and approaches which are of major benefit to people in all walks of life, including business, sales, management, sport, health, education, coaching, therapy and every aspect of human endeavour where there is some form of communication.

SOME BACKGROUND AND HISTORY OF NLP

NLP was originally developed by John Grinder and Richard Bandler in the mid 1970s. Grinder was a professor of linguistics at University of California, Santa Cruz. Bandler was a student of mathematics. They teamed up to investigate the types of language and linguistic patterns used by effective psychotherapists. In particular, they 'modelled' three therapists – Fritz Perls, Virginia Satir and Milton Erickson. Modelling is a term frequently used in NLP. In essence modelling is finding out what and how someone does something, normally a behaviour that the modeller would like to emulate. A more detailed definition is given in the glossary (see p.245).

Now in case you are wondering why it would be useful to you to read anything about psychotherapy (apologies to any therapists reading this), think of it this way: therapists are in the business of communication and persuasion, persuading people to change behaviour patterns and responses that they may have done for most of their life. So, if effective use of language can help people change ingrained behaviours, it will probably be valuable in helping the vast majority of people to improve their communication and make changes to their own behaviours.

Bandler and Grinder were curious about what was the difference that made the difference between good therapists/communicators, and these three excellent ones. In modelling these therapists, Bandler and Grinder initially developed a set of language patterns that are extremely useful when communicating.

As a result of this initial modelling project, and their curiosity about 'what's the difference that makes the difference' between someone who is excellent and someone who is 'merely' very good, they and other people after them have developed more and more 'techniques' which we now know as NLP.

The question 'what's the difference that makes the difference?' is an important one, because it can inform us about the changes we could make to improve what we do. If we perform well in certain situations, how do we do that? How can we replicate that in other situations to improve 'performance' (whether it is selling, presenting, playing sport, teaching, asking our children to do something or asking for a pay increase)?

Because NLP is an art and a science, there are differing views about certain aspects of NLP within the NLP community. So if you hear or read about slightly different points of view, or different ways to express some NLP concepts, just consider that your toolkit has been enriched, so that you can use the technique(s) that seem most appropriate to the situation at the time.

THE BENEFITS OF NLP

There are three main benefits of NLP. NLP helps us to:

- Improve communication
- Change our behaviours and beliefs
- 'Model' excellence, in other words if we (or someone else) can do something really well, how do we (or they) do it, and how can we (or they) replicate it when we (or they) want/need to?

Let's explore each benefit in turn.

Improving communication

Communication is probably the most fundamental aspect of human interaction. Have you ever 'communicated' with someone, thinking that you both knew what each other meant, and afterwards you were surprised at their interpretation, or they were surprised at yours, or both? Or have you said the same thing to two people, and one responded in one way while the other person responded completely differently?

NLP provides us with a set of communication tools which will significantly reduce the likelihood of misunderstandings (no, it can't completely remove this likelihood. Better results faster? Yes. Miracles? No). We will cover these communication tools in Parts 2 and 4.

In addition to communicating with others, we also communicate with ourselves. If you think we don't communicate with ourselves, what was it you just said to yourself when you read this last sentence? When you do something really well, what do you say to yourself? And if you do something you regret, such as making a mistake during a presentation, or dropping the milk on the kitchen floor, you will probably say something to yourself (out loud or in your head, or both). Given that we communicate with ourselves, how can we improve the way we do so to improve our results? NLP offers some ways to do that.

Changing behaviours and changing beliefs

As we will discover in Part 3, there are numerous methods in NLP to help change our behaviours if we find those behaviours are not giving us the results we want. And as we shall see in Chapters 3 (p.37) and 8 (p.119), our behaviours are strongly influenced by our beliefs. Sometimes people have beliefs which are not useful, such as, 'I can't become a good salesperson', or 'I can't become a good athlete', or 'I have to know all the answers when making a presentation'. NLP has numerous ways to help people change their beliefs and behaviours.

Modelling excellence

Finding out how someone does something is fundamental to NLP. How does an excellent golfer know exactly how to make the putt, and what does he/she do that is different from someone who is merely a good player? How does an excellent salesperson know when to close the deal? How does an excellent teacher know that the students have learned the topic before moving on to the next topic? What are some of our own strategies for excellence, and how can we replicate those consistently, and possibly even apply the same process in other contexts? NLP provides many of the answers to these questions, and provides a methodology to model excellence. Although the full process of modelling is outside the scope of this book, we will cover some important aspects of modelling.

SOME OF THE MAIN USES OF NLP

Given the three main benefits of NLP, it can be used in virtually every area of life. Here are some specific ways, many of which will be covered in detail in this book. Those aspects in *italicised text* are unfortunately outside the scope of this book, and are included purely so that you know of the breadth of possibilities offered by using NLP.

Business/work
- Sales
- Advertising and marketing
- Managing people
- Building customer relations and/or supplier relations
- Negotiation
- Conflict/dispute resolution
- Team-building
- Leadership
- Presentations
- Recruitment
- Interviews
- Creative problem solving
- Improved decision-making

Coaching
- Helping clients achieve goals
- Increasing overall fulfilment
- Feeling more confident
- Overcoming personal barriers to success

Education
- Learning
- Teaching
- *Learning 'problems' eg 'poor' spelling*

Health
- *Weight loss*
- *Overcoming illness*
- *Eating disorders*
- *Anxiety*
- *Allergies*
- *Quitting smoking*
- *Phobias*

Sport
- Improving focus
- Overcoming bad performances
- Feeling confident, and/or overcoming nerves
- Mental rehearsal/visualisation

Relationships
- Finding a suitable partner
- Improving communications within families

NLP can also be used therapeutically, although such uses are outside the scope of this book.

Some of the uses of NLP listed above under certain headings can apply to other headings, for example better decision-making could be used in any area of one's life, team-building could be used in sport, etc.

✐ ACTION POINT

Referring to the main uses of NLP from above, make a list of things in your life that you would like to change. As you read this book, use the relevant topics to assist you in making the changes you want.

WHAT IS NLP NOT?

A word of caution about NLP. NLP has a hugely powerful set of tools to help people change the way they think. It can also be used to influence other people. Therefore, like any powerful tool, it is essential to treat it with respect and to use the techniques to create 'win-win' situations. In NLP, we often refer the concept of Ecology. Ecology in this context relates to considering the implications of any changes you make or actions you take on the wider system, be it other aspects of your own life or the impact on others. For example, if you want to make changes in your career, what could be the impact on your health, your relationships, and on those close to you such as partners or children? We will consider ecology further in Chapter 4 (p.51).

Occasionally I hear people say that NLP is 'manipulative'. Techniques cannot be manipulative; it is only the intention of the individual that can cause a technique to be misused. Is a surgeon's scalpel dangerous? In the right hands, it saves lives. In the wrong hands.... Therefore, I request that you use the information in this book wisely and ethically.

Moreover, as mentioned already, NLP is **not** a substitute for therapy or counselling if that is what someone requires. Similarly, even though it has applications in the field of health, it is **not** a substitute for suitably qualified medical advice.

QUICK RECAP

- *NLP provides a set of powerful tools to help you to change the way you think and give you the edge in certain situations, so that you can have more of what you want and less of what you don't want.*
- *It can be used in numerous situations and different areas of life.*
- *It helps people to communicate more effectively, change behaviours and beliefs, and to 'model' or replicate excellence more consistently and in other situations.*
- *It is **not** a substitute for appropriate medical or therapeutic treatment.*
- *It is used most effectively when seeking win-win situations.*

CHAPTER 2

Communication: what happens inside our mind?

Have you ever wondered why people perceive things differently? Why is it that two people can see the same film and have different views, thoughts and feelings about it, or that two interviewers may have different opinions about a candidate? Why is it that two golfers will respond differently to a delay caused by the weather? Why is it that a couple will walk down a road, one will notice the cars and the other will notice the clothes people are wearing?

Many of these questions can be answered by the model of communication used in NLP. It is important to stress that this is just that, *a* model, not *the* model, nor a statement of truth.

OVERVIEW OF THE COMMUNICATION MODEL

Take a look at the diagram of the Communication Model below.
To make it really easy to follow, assume that the elements to the
right of the face denote external events, and the elements 'inside'
the head denote what happens literally inside someone's head.

NLP COMMUNICATION MODEL

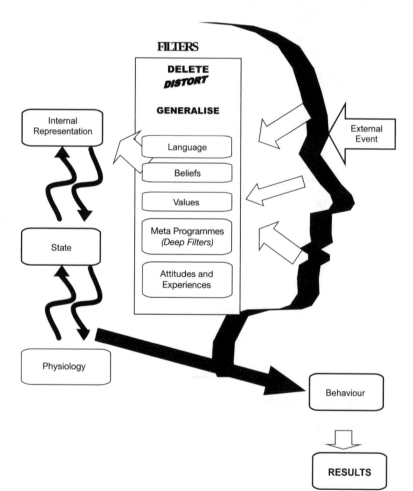

Starting from the right, each external event is an 'information stimulus', which we perceive through our five senses: sight (visual), hearing (auditory), feel (kinaesthetic), smell (olfactory) and taste (gustatory). In NLP these senses are referred to as Representational Systems, in other words how we represent the external world internally. We will explore these further in Chapter 6 (p.81).

These 'stimuli' are then filtered internally to produce an Internal Representation or mental image of what we *think* we have perceived through our representational systems. We will discuss these filters in the next section.

This mental image will impact on our State; if we have 'pleasant' mental images of what we perceive, we will probably feel content, happy or some other 'positive' state. Equally, if we have 'unpleasant' mental images, we may feel upset in some way (angry, anxious, etc).

Depending on whether we are in a good state or not, this will be reflected in our 'physiology', such as our posture and our breathing.

Mental images/internal representations, state and physiology are inter-related. For example, we can change our physiology as a way to change our state and internal representations. It is not unknown for psychotherapists to prescribe exercise for people who are depressed; the exercise is a change of physiology, which changes their state and therefore their mental images. All sports people will know the highs and positivity they feel after a hard training session. Even standing upright, smiling, with your shoulders back will probably improve the way you are feeling compared to slouching, looking down and having a frown on your face.

Internal representations, state and physiology are important because they impact on our *behaviours*, and our behaviours impact on our *results*.

ACTION POINT

Pick someone who you know very well, and who you see frequently (partner, family member, colleague, friend, team-mate). Notice how you notice whether he/she is in a good mood or a bad mood. Make a mental note of the physiological signs – posture, facial expression, voice inflexion – you pick up on. Whatever you notice, remember that our physiology and our state are linked. We will expand on this in Chapter 5 (p.69).

THE THREE MAIN FILTERS

Let's now consider in more detail the key aspects of what happens inside people's minds, starting with the three main filters, namely Deletion, Distortion and Generalisation. We will then consider some of the determinants of what information we delete, distort and generalise.

Deletion

It has been estimated that there are millions of 'bits' of 'information stimuli' happening to us each second. In his book *Flow* (Harper Perennial, 2008), Professor Mihaly Csikszentmihalyi estimated that we are only consciously aware of around 126 bits per second. Therefore, there is a lot of information being deleted. Even if these numbers are exaggerated, you probably weren't aware of the feeling of your legs against the chair you're probably sitting on until you read this sentence, or of the texture of the pages against your fingers or of the sound of the people around you, or of the material of the clothes you're wearing right now. Indeed, psychologists have asserted that if we were simultaneously aware of all of the information and events that were happening we'd go insane. To avoid this we only focus on some of the information and events, so, when we go into a crowded room, for example, we delete some of the sounds so that we can tune in to the conversation we're having.

So we delete a huge amount of infomation (did you spot the deletion – the 'r' was deleted from 'information') from our conscious awareness. Please note there is a difference between deleting and ignoring (for example, requests to do household chores or homework).

Putting humour to one side for a moment, deletion is not a good or bad thing – it's just what we humans do. How can you use this knowledge usefully? One way is to be aware that people you communicate with may inadvertently delete some of the information that you tell them. Hence, it may be useful to check that people have seen/heard what you wanted them to see/hear. For parents, when giving important information to your children (for example about safety), you might want to check they have understood it and remembered *all* of it. For bosses, when briefing colleagues or staff members about important issues, it may be useful to check they have understood it all.

Another factor to take into account when communicating is the notion of Chunking. According to Princeton University Professor George Miller's study in 1956, people are able to handle between five and nine 'chunks' of information at a time before becoming overwhelmed. Miller also discovered that we can increase this amount if we organise it into appropriate chunks or groupings of information. We will come back to this topic in Chapter 7 (p.93).

TOP TIPS

When communicating, recognise that people may be able to handle only limited pieces of information at a time. Keep it simple and to the point when giving instructions, especially when there is some pressure, for example during a half-time team talk, or when managers give a sales pep-talk before a busy day in the department store. Also remember that for some of the people you are giving instructions to, some of their five to nine chunks of attention may be directed elsewhere. I am reminded of the phrase often used by my first NLP trainer – 'less is more'.

Distortion

We all ditsort (did you spot the distortion?) information in our minds. As with deletions, this is not good or bad – it's just what we do. Examples of commonplace distortions are:

- When we shop for clothes, we mentally compare what we are seeing externally to the memory of what we have in our wardrobe to see if the new clothes will match what we already have

- When we look to buy a property, we imagine the rooms being decorated in a certain way

- Sports players visualising their desired performance before an event, or coaches planning a particular move or tactic

- Thinking that the doorbell or phone has rung when we're in the shower, even though it has not

- Imagining that our boss or colleague is annoyed with us just because they didn't say 'hello' at the coffee machine this morning

Distortions can be limiting or useful. For example:

- In work, are you blowing out of proportion the error you made when presenting last month's figures and hence putting unnecessary additional pressure on yourself, or are you putting the mistake into perspective so that it merely informs you about what to do differently to improve yet does not adversely impact on your next presentation?

- In sport, are you building your opponents up to be something they are not, hence 'psyching yourself out', or are you 'cutting them down to size' in your mind?

- In your personal life, have your friends really stopped calling you as often as they did, or does it just seem that way? And even if they have stopped calling as often, does it mean that they're giving you the cold shoulder, or could it be that they are just really busy?

TOP TIPS

As human beings, we are 'meaning making machines', ie we make meaning of and interpret the events in our life. Notice the meaning you place on events, and distinguish the facts from your interpretation or distortions. If you think that, for example, your boss is annoyed with you because she didn't speak to you at the coffee machine, don't let it fester, simply check it out. She could simply have a lot on her mind.

Generalisation

A generalisation is when we take one piece of data or information and assume that other things within that category are the same or that the pattern will be repeated. Generalisations can be extremely useful when learning – for example if I learn the principles of how to add up 13 plus 24, I can generalise the principles to be able to add up 27 plus 35. If I can drive one car, I can drive other cars.

As with deletions and distortions, generalisations can be either useful or limiting. They are the basis of 'isms' such as racism, sexism, ageism, where someone assumes (generalises) that because one or some people in a particular category of people may behave in a certain way, all people in that category will do so. Not all generalisations are negative though.

Some useful generalisations in different contexts could be, for example:

- 'When I train hard at the gym I feel more energised at work, and I have been training hard recently so I am confident that I will perform at my best in tomorrow's assessment centre.'

- 'Because I/we have won the last three matches against this team/opponent, I/we will win today' (but watch for over-confidence).

- 'I worked hard and passed my last set of exams with excellent grades, and because I have worked hard this time, I will get excellent grades again.'

Here are some examples of generalisations which may be limiting:

- 'I find it hard to play against left-handers, and my opponent today is a leftie so it's going to be tough today.'

- 'I froze in my last two interviews and so I may well do so in next week's interview.'

- 'My last relationship ended badly, so I'm not very good at relationships.'

You have probably noticed that many of the generalisations expressed above take the form of 'beliefs'. That's because beliefs are often little more than generalisations, and the following exercise will give you a very clear experience of that. This is a simple example of how generalisations can lead to beliefs. Please do this exercise now before you read any further:

ACTION POINT

Imagine that you've set your alarm clock for 7.30am. You have a big day, full of important meetings at work. The alarm goes off, and you switch on the radio and hear the DJ say it's 7.55, and you realise that you made a mistake setting the alarm clock. You start rushing around and stub your foot on the bedside table, hobble to the wardrobe to find that your favourite shirt/blouse that you always wear for important days has a stain on it. When you get to the kitchen to make your regular morning coffee you notice there is none left.
What do you believe about that day?

The chances are that you think 'it's going to be a bad day', or something similar. Some of you may think 'it can only get better', but generally the former will be the most common response. Now here's the important point – you generalised this information and formed this belief based on up to four selected pieces of information (some of you formed the belief after one or two pieces), and this belief could turn into a self-fulfilling prophecy.

While the example above is relatively trivial, the same principles apply to beliefs that are more limiting.

We all delete, distort and generalise the information that comes to us. We will now consider the factors determining **what** we delete, distort and generalise.

THE DETERMINANTS OF THE MAIN FILTERS

There are several filters which determine what we delete, distort and generalise. Let's briefly consider them.

Language

Language is fascinating. The words we use, both externally to other people and internally to ourselves (the vast majority of us talk to ourselves inside our heads), can determine and even define our experience. If we do not have words for a particular event or feeling, how can we express it? Does that event or feeling actually exist? I have trained several people in NLP who are either bilingual or very proficient in more than one language, and they all say that their world is different depending on which language they are talking.

Another way of demonstrating the impact that language has on our thinking is as follows. Consider the two following sentences:

1. 'I can't do XXX (speak in public/sing/hit a topspin backhand etc).'

2. 'I haven't yet learned how to do XXX (speak in public/sing/ hit a topspin backhand etc) as well I as would like.'

For most people, the first sentence disempowers, creating a negative internal representation/mental image, whereas the second creates possibilities. Changing the way we 'language' situations will change the meaning we place on them and hence the internal representation(s) we have.

✊ ACTION POINT

Pick something that you could insert to replace XXX in the two sentences on the previous page, and say both of the sentences. Notice the impact of the first statement; then notice the impact of the second. Which do you prefer? Which is more empowering?

TOP TIPS

Pay attention to the way you express your thoughts, especially ones which limit you. Find a way to express these thoughts in a more useful way. Please note this does not mean pretending problems do not exist, or burying your head in the sand. It simply means choosing your words wisely.

We will cover more about language in Chapters 6 (p.81) and 7 (p.93).

Beliefs

Beliefs is another filter, and can be defined in several ways, for example:

• Our current thinking about a particular topic

• Those convictions and opinions that we hold to be true

We all have beliefs. When other people have beliefs, especially when they differ from ours, we tend to call them 'opinions', but when we believe something we often call it 'fact' or 'truth'. Richard Bandler (one of the co-developers of NLP) comments that people are addicted to their beliefs. We only have to look at some of the problems caused by religious beliefs to notice evidence of this – people are willing to kill and die for their beliefs rather than consider the possibility that there may be other ways to interpret or consider events.

From the point of view of the NLP Communication Model and the filters, if we believe something is true, we will often filter out (ie delete, distort or generalise) information that contradicts it, or distort information so that it fits in with our beliefs. You will have heard the saying 'I'll believe it when I see it'. Consider that a more appropriate saying is 'I'll see it when I believe it'.

To illustrate this, let me refer to a client:

Q EXAMPLE

Jane was a director of a successful HR consultancy. During a coaching session, she confided that she did not believe she could sell. Knowing that she had sold deals worth millions of pounds (otherwise she would not have made it to director level) I asked her to give me an example of a large sale she had made. After several moments of silence and protests, she begrudgingly mentioned a particular blue-chip client to whom she had sold around £500,000. I then asked for another example, and only marginally quicker came a similar response. We continued to do this exercise for up to 10 times, by which time she had finally convinced herself that the belief she had was not actually true.

Afterwards, given that Jane's beliefs had changed, she was able to internalise events in a way that helped her have a more realistic assessment of her capabilities, ie that she really could sell effectively. This also helped her to have positive mental images before attending sales meetings, which helped her be in a confident state, which helped her sell more, and so it became a virtuous circle.

From the Communication Model perspective, because Jane's beliefs had changed, her internal representations, state and physiology changed both before and during sales meetings, hence her behaviours and results changed.

A more well-known example is that of Sir Roger Bannister and the four-minute mile. Some medical experts 'knew' that it was medically unsafe for anyone to run a mile in less than four minutes (note they didn't 'believe' it, they 'knew' it). However, once the barrier had been broken, it was broken numerous times that year. Athletes' beliefs had changed, leading to a change in their internal representations about the mile, the state and physiology they were in and hence a change in their behaviours and therefore results.

As Henry Ford said, 'whether you believe you can or believe you can't, you're right'. In other words, our beliefs determine what can and cannot do.

Values

Values is another important filter. From an NLP perspective, values can be defined as 'what is important to us', or 'what we want or seek', in any particular context. For example, if one of our values in a career context is 'challenge', we will seek tasks and situations which challenge us. If one of our values in the context of relationships is 'fun', we will seek people and situations where we can have fun.

Generally, values have two main functions:

- They determine how we spend our time and direct our energies; we tend to do things which are important to us, and not do things which aren't important to us.

- They determine how we feel about what we have done afterwards. Most of us have probably done things which we regret because they 'go against the grain'.

You have probably realised from this that values are key elements of our motivation – we will generally be motivated to do or have the things that are important to us, and not be motivated to do or have things which aren't important to us. Values are also extremely useful when selling, managing, recruiting and making choices, and will be covered in more detail in Chapter 13 (p.181).

From the Communication Model perspective, if a piece of 'information stimuli' is important to us, we will probably pay attention to it; if it isn't, we probably will not. For example, as a former finance director of a restaurant chain, often when I go to restaurants I will notice the number of people in the restaurant (to make an estimate of whether they are making money – sad but true). My friends will pay attention to different events, for example the clothes people are wearing, the conversations at other tables or the feel of the restaurant, because *that* is what is important to *them*. The same events are present, but our values influence what and how we delete, distort and generalise.

Meta Programmes

Meta Programmes is NLP jargon for filters which in effect sit beyond, or underpin, other filters. They are deeply embedded filters which operate irrespective of the content of what's happening. For this reason we will refer to them as Deep Filters. It is generally accepted in NLP that there are around 15–20 of these deep filters. For each of the deep filters, we will all be somewhere along a spectrum for that filter. This will be explained in more detail in Chapter 14 (p.195).

To illustrate briefly let me give you an example of one of the deep filters known as the 'direction filter'. People can either be motivated *towards* what they want or *away from* what they don't want, or somewhere along the spectrum of the two. The two ends of this particular spectrum are sometimes known as the 'carrot or stick'.

In any given context, for example work, some people will direct their energy *towards* what they want (for example 'being successful', increasing sales by x%), whereas others will focus their energy on avoiding (moving *away from*) what they don't want (presumably 'not failing' or 'not stagnating'), regardless of the specific content of the external situation. By knowing about our and other people's deep filters, we can gain greater insight into our own and other people's behaviours and responses to situations, and therefore be better able to influence others.

ATTITUDES AND EXPERIENCES

From an NLP perspective, Attitudes are simply a collection of beliefs and values about a particular subject. The experiences we have will often create values, beliefs and attidudes.

A WORD ABOUT OUR 'MINDS'

Before we move on to the next topic, it is important to say a few words about our 'minds'. In NLP, there is the concept of our 'conscious' mind and our 'unconscious/sub-conscious' mind. Many books have been written on these subjects, and I would like to summarise this concept in just a few paragraphs.

Our conscious mind holds what we are aware of consciously at any one moment. Our unconscious mind holds everything else, and has different levels. So even though you were probably not consciously thinking about your mobile phone number until you just read this sentence, the information was close to the surface of your unconscious mind and may have been quickly transferred into your conscious mind if you wanted it.

Put simplistically, the purpose of the conscious mind is to set goals and to think rationally, rather like the captain of a ship. The purpose of the unconscious mind is to make happen what the conscious mind wants, rather like the crew of the ship. When you drive, ride a bike, and walk down the road, you almost certainly do it automatically, ie your unconscious mind does it for you.

Within the unconscious mind are different levels – the more surface level (which stores information like your mobile phone number) and deeper levels, which store many of our memories. If we think back to the Communication Model, of the millions of bits of information that we receive every second, we are consciously aware of only 126 bits. Where do all the other bits go? That's right, into your unconscious. That is why we hear of people who, if they see professional hypnotherapists, are able to recollect lots of memories when in a trance (ie when their unconscious mind is accessed), memories which they cannot remember when in their normal waking state. And from a scientific point of view, Michael Talbot in his book *The Holographic Universe* (HarperCollins, 1996), refers to Wilder Penfield, a Canadian neurosurgeon. Penfield postulated that all the memories of everything that has ever happened to us are stored within us.

For more information, there are numerous books available on the subject of hypnosis which will give a far more in-depth insight into the unconscious mind. Some of these are listed in the *References and further reading* section.

The impact of the Communication Model

So given that we all have different experiences, beliefs, values, deep filters profile, attitudes, experiences and ways in which we use language, it is not surprising that there are misunderstandings when people communicate, and that we have different opinions and notice different things about a given event. If an independent researcher asked you to give detailed feedback on what you have gleaned from this book, it is almost certain that your 'feedback' would be different from every other reader, even though the external events (ie the words of this book) are the same. When you listen to sports commentators analysing a sporting event, or political commentators analysing the political situation, even though they will have seen the same match, or heard the same political speeches, their analyses will differ.

QUICK RECAP

- *We all filter out externally generated information to provide ourselves with an Internal Representation, or rather an 'internal re-presentation' of what we think we have experienced through our five senses.*
- *The key filter processes are Deletion, Distortion and Generalisation, based on our language, beliefs, values, attitudes, experiences and Deep Filters.*
- *Given that we all filter differently, it's useful for us to understand what Internal Representations other people may have formed from our communication, so that we can adjust our approach and communication accordingly.*
- *It is also useful to accept that we do not always make useful Internal Representations from other people's communications. By being aware of this, we can begin to examine our responses, and use some of the NLP skills available to seek alternative ways to respond.*

CHAPTER 3

The mindset for success: the fundamental attitudes within NLP

The early developers of NLP found that successful people had certain key attitudes and beliefs that helped them to succeed, regardless of the field of activity. They used these as a basis to develop the NLP techniques that we use today. Two key aspects of the foundations upon which NLP is built are:

- The Principles for Success
- The NLP Presuppositions (ie fundamental beliefs and premises) – 'The mindset for success'

This chapter discusses some of the fundamental principles of NLP and how to apply them in everyday life.

THE PRINCIPLES FOR SUCCESS

There are six Principles for Success:

1. Know what you want (know your 'outcome')

2. Be aware of what is happening and of your progress so that you can get feedback

3. Be flexible if what you are doing is not working as you would like

4. Build and maintain rapport

5. Operate from a physiology and psychology of excellence

6. Take action

Each of these is a separate topic in and of itself, and is covered in more detail later in the book. We will look at each of these briefly in turn here.

As you read through these please remember that even if some of these seem obvious to you, sometimes we ignore the obvious.

Know what you want

It is really useful to know what you want before beginning any activity. The concept of outcomes and goals is a big one, and the whole of Chapter 4 (p.51) is devoted to this topic. It is sufficient to say at this juncture that a trait of successful people is that they know exactly what they want. I would urge everyone to always begin a task knowing what they want from it. This includes not just big aspects of the goal (for example, becoming the human resources director of a FTSE 100 company; becoming a judo black belt) but also specific tasks, for example meetings at work and specific training sessions in sport.

Q EXAMPLE

*A tri-athlete client improved her performance significantly by being absolutely clear what her targets were for each training session **before** each session, and how these targets fitted in with, and would help her reach, her overall triathlon goals.*

Be aware, take feedback

Notice what results you're getting. Notice what works, and what doesn't work. By being aware of the results you are getting you can change things if you are not getting the results you want; you can do more of what works and stop doing what doesn't work.

Similarly when having a meeting or conversation with a colleague or friend, if you have your awareness on the other person you will notice whether the points you want to make are being 'received' by the other person. In Chapter 5 (p.69), we will take a look at some of the tools available in NLP which help people to assess whether their message is being received as intended.

Be flexible

If the feedback you are getting suggests that you are not on track, it will almost certainly be worthwhile making changes to bring you back on track rather than repeating the same unsuccessful behaviours. Knowing exactly what to do differently may or may not be obvious, but at least you can direct your efforts into finding something that could work, perhaps something that does work for someone else, or some other possible different approach. This is where being flexible matters. Sometimes it's important to be very flexible, to be willing to think outside the box.

Build and maintain rapport

Rapport is a term used in NLP to describe a feeling of mutual trust between two or more people. The deeper the rapport, the better the relationship and the more likely it is people will follow your requests. It is hard to imagine being able to achieve anything worthwhile, or to have fulfilling relationships, if you cannot build trust and rapport; hence much of Chapter 5 (p.69) is devoted to how to build rapport with people.

Operate from a physiology and psychology of excellence

Quite simply, think positive thoughts and use body movements and posture that are appropriate for someone seeking excellent results. Our mind and body are linked – this will be further explained later in the section on presuppositions of NLP (p.41). And remembering back to Chapter 2, and the diagram showing the Communication Model (p.20), we know there is a link between physiology and the mind.

🔍 EXAMPLE

I use an exercise on my training courses to demonstrate the mind-body link. I ask delegates to hold out their right arm in front of them, parallel to the ground and turn clockwise as far as they comfortably can (or their left arm and turn anti-clockwise), and to make a mental note of where their index finger is pointing (I ask them to take care or even not to do this exercise if they have any back problems). I then ask them to stand as they normally would, and to imagine their arm turning just one inch further than it was, and that it is easy, comfortable, and they are relaxed. I repeat this, increasing it incrementally until they are imagining pointing one or two feet further round than they were, again it is easy, they are comfortable and relaxed. I ask them to hold in mind however far round they saw themselves turning, and to keep the comfortable feelings and any associated sounds. I then ask them to open their eyes and turn and notice how far round they go. Around 95% of the delegates turn significantly further. They changed the way they thought about it, and the physical results changed.

As for the 'psychology of excellence', much of this book concentrates on NLP techniques which help people have a positive mindset and to think in ways which help them to achieve better results faster.

Take action

Yes, it is obvious that we need to take action in order to make changes. But do you do take action? Always? Are there things you know you should do (for example, going to the gym) yet you do not do it?

Q EXAMPLE

In the late 1990's a friend of mine worked for an organisation providing personal development courses. During the sessions which introduced the concepts to potential delegates, he would always ask, 'how many of you know of something you could do to improve your life and yet you don't do it?' Virtually everyone would raise their hands.

TOP TIPS

Use the Principles for Success in your life. Always know what you want from an activity before you start, take feedback on your progress, make changes if you're not on target, build good relations with people, think and act positively, and take whatever action (within reason) is required to achieve your goal.

NLP PRESUPPOSITIONS – THE MINDSET FOR SUCCESS

The second of the two aspects of the foundations upon which NLP is built are known as the NLP Presuppositions. These are a series of convenient beliefs and assumptions (as opposed to 'truths') which, when people assume and act as if they are true, usually help people to produce better results in whatever field of endeavour they are applied.

As I mentioned earlier in this book, there are different 'schools' of NLP, and some have a slightly different view about these presuppositions. I will list some of the presuppositions and the interpretation which I have found to be most useful. Please also note that these presuppositions are often useful when taken together, not just in isolation, and remember to apply common sense.

Here is a summary of the presuppositions we will cover:

- Have respect for other people's point of view.

- The meaning and outcome of communication is in the response you get.

- There is no failure, just feedback.

- Flexibility rules, OK!

- We all have untapped potential to achieve more.

- We are making the best choices we believe are available.

- Modelling excellence leads to improved performance.

- The mind and body affect each other.

- The 'map' is not the 'territory'.

Have respect for other people's point of view

We are all different from other people. As we discussed in Chapter 2 (p.19), we have all had different backgrounds and experiences, and have formed different beliefs and attitudes as a result of these and consequently will have different points of view and opinions.

By recognising that there are differences, and respecting these different points of view, we can form the foundations of co-operation. Respecting someone's point of view does *not* mean that we agree with it, or like it, or accept it is valid for us. It simply means that we can honour where someone is 'coming from'.

Think of it from your own perspective. If, during a debate or even a disagreement, you believe and feel that the other person is hearing you and respecting your point of view (even though they don't agree with it), you will probably be far more likely to want to interact and co-operate with them and to feel respectful towards them, compared to if you feel that they are *not* respectful of your point of view.

Stephen Covey, in his best-selling book *The 7 Habits of Highly Successful People* (Simon & Schuster, 2004), states that one of the habits is 'seek first to understand, then be understood' which seems very similar to 'have respect for other people's point of view'.

Throughout this book there will be ideas of how you can see other perspectives, and in Chapter 11 (p.161) we will be covering a specific NLP technique to help you do this.

The meaning and outcome of communication is in the response you get

We may believe that by clearly communicating our thoughts and feelings through words other people should understand our meaning.

However, they will respond to what *they* think you said, not what *you* think you've said (remember the Communication Model). You can determine how effectively you are communicating by the response you get from the person you are communicating with. In addition, if by some chance someone responds to you in a way that is not what you intended, you can recognise that it is for you to alter your communication rather than wait for (or expect) others to change. When we accept this presupposition we are able to take 100% responsibility for all of our communication rather than adopt a 'blame' approach.

There is no failure, just feedback

If a person does not succeed in something, this does not mean they have failed. They simply have not succeeded *yet*. It may be useful for them to do something differently to find a different way of achieving their outcome. This links to one of the Principles for Success (flexibility) mentioned earlier, and to the next presupposition.

According to Jeff Grout and Sarah Perrin, authors of *Mind Games* (Capstone, 2006), Roger Black MBE, the 400m champion at World and European Games, spent much of his career thinking about what would happen if he didn't succeed. He finally realised that there was no such thing as failure, and when he knew that, he could perform the way he wanted without feeling pressure.

According to Napoleon Hill, author of *Think and Grow Rich* (originally published in 1937), Thomas Edison, the inventor of the light-bulb, attempted to create it 10,000 times before it actually worked. Did he 'fail' 10,000 times? In Edison's mind, it was simply feedback that what he was doing did not work; indeed, according to Hill, Edison believed that each 'non-success' was taking him closer to success.

Flexibility rules, OK!

The person(s) with the most flexibility (choices) of behaviour will have the most influence on the situation. What this means is that the more options you have in your situation the more likely it is that you will get the result you want. A salesman with only three ways to approach customers will almost certainly sell less than a salesman with equivalent ability and experience who has 103 ways to approach customers. In business and work, the ability of organisations to adapt to changing economic environments and markets is essential.

If we extend this to communication, the more ways we have to communicate our ideas, the more likely we are to be able to alter a person's perceptions and actions.

We all have untapped potential to achieve more

People themselves are not un-resourceful. They may be experiencing un-resourceful states (as mentioned early in Chapter 2 (p.19), our state is how we are feeling emotionally at any given moment). When we change from an un-resourceful state (such as anxiety) to a more positive state (such as confidence), we then have access to the potential within us to accomplish far more than we can when we are feeling in an un-resourceful state (we will cover how to change states in Chapter 9 (p.133). Even if someone does not have the specific skills/attributes at the moment to achieve a specific goal, they do have the ability to gain the skills.

We are making the best choices we believe are available

People are making the best choices they can given their 'point of view' or 'model of the world'. People may occasionally behave in ways which seem ridiculous to on-lookers and even to themselves in the cold light of day. Yet if we can bear in mind that all behaviours have a positive intention for that person, and that people are doing the best they can do at the time with the options they believe are available to them, it helps us to have compassion for people when they appear to be acting in ways that are inappropriate. Please consider that their present behaviour is the best choice they believe is available at the time, and has a positive intent for them. Why would anyone do anything that wasn't the best choice they believed they had available at the time?

Modelling excellence leads to improved performance

Modelling is the process used by Bandler and Grinder in developing NLP. By modelling someone's excellence, improvements can be made by taking the best from the best.

ACTION POINT

Pick a capability you have that you would like to improve. Examples could be selling, a particular sport, telling jokes, remembering people's names and so on. Find someone who does what you want to do, or a particular aspect of it, really well. Notice what he/she does that you don't, and what you do that he/she doesn't, with a view to improving what you do. If you have the opportunity and it is appropriate to do so, ask them how they do it.

Remember that we have excellent capabilities which we could utilise in other areas. For example, if we are excellent at remembering phone numbers, how do we do it, and how could we replicate that strategy to, for example, remember names? Sometimes it is useful to break down tasks into 'bite-size chunks', which can make 'difficult' tasks that are done with apparent ease by experts seem easier for us to do.

ACTION POINT

Pick some capabilities you have and 'get curious' about how you could use them in other contexts.

The mind and body affect each other

As we discussed in Chapter 2 (p.19) and as shown by the experience of my course delegates turning their arm further than they thought possible, the mind and the body are one unit, interconnected. Changes in one will normally have an impact on the other. There are numerous examples, including from the worlds of medicine and sport, where changes in one's mental approach yield changes in physical results and vice versa. We have probably all heard of the term 'psychosomatic illness', (where illnesses are brought on by stress or other psychological factors) and the 'placebo effect' is well-documented (a placebo is a neutral substance given to a patient under the pretence that they are receiving a proven or active drug. Often patients' health will improve because they believe the 'drug' will work).

In the world of sport, the performance of many competitors will be changed when they are 'under pressure'. Pressure is all in the mind.

The 'map' is not the 'territory'

We could consider that the external world is the 'territory', and that the way people internalise it is their 'map' of what the territory is. People will respond to their 'map' of what they think is 'reality', not to 'reality' or the 'territory' itself. We all have different maps of what we think is real – that is one explanation of why we respond differently compared to other people in response to a given situation.

As you will remember from the NLP Communication Model, we create our own reality based on, among other things, our past experiences and beliefs. One way of looking at and describing NLP is that it is the art of changing our 'map' to create more choices.

⚡ ACTION POINT

Pick some situations in your life where you were successful. Which of the NLP presuppositions were you operating from (whether you knew it or not)? Pick some situations where you were not so successful. Which NLP presuppositions would have helped had you known them at the time?

CAUSE AND EFFECT, RESULTS AND REASONS

The topics covered in this chapter can be usefully summed up by the concept of 'cause and effect'. In essence, we can either be 'at effect' of some 'cause' over which we have no control and which 'makes' us respond in some negative way, or we can be 'at cause', which means we take 100% responsibility for the results we currently have in our life and for making changes to our situation and to our responses, so that we can have more of what we want and less of what we don't want.

If we are 'at effect' we tend to make excuses, have lots of really good 'reasons' for not getting the results we want in our career, relationships and life generally, and generally don't get enough of what we want. When we are 'at cause', we take full responsibility for what happens in our life and the way we respond to it; we take the necessary action to achieve what we want and make no excuses, and tend to get better results than if we were 'at effect'.

Yes, maybe our sector of the economy is a little slow. Maybe the teacher isn't as good as the one we had last year. Maybe our team hasn't been getting the rub of the green recently. Maybe I should have got that promotion. So what? If we make excuses and moan, how does that help us compared to if we turned any perceived negatives into positives?

Clearly even with an 'at cause' attitude we may not always get the results we want in the short term. However, people who are 'at cause' will usually get better results over the long term than those who are 'at effect' by taking responsibility for making changes in their life. In the rest of the book we will explore tips and techniques that can help you do this, based on these NLP beliefs.

QUICK RECAP

- *Operate from the Principles for Success.*
- *Always start with the goal in mind.*
- *Notice whether you're on track to get the results you want.*
- *Be flexible enough to change if you are not on track.*
- *Take action!*
- *Learn and operate from the NLP Presuppositions – they work.*
- *Notice when you are 'at cause' and 'at effect'. If ever you are 'at effect', ask yourself how you can move to being 'at cause'.*

CHAPTER 4

Your goals:
how to set and achieve them

Remembering back to the Principles for Success, having a goal in mind is essential before starting any task. Many people do not set goals at all. Those who do often set them in such a way that is not 100% conducive to achieving them. This chapter will provide you with NLP techniques for setting goals, so that it is much more likely that you will achieve them.

WHY SET GOALS?

The three main reasons for setting effective goals are:

- It provides a sense of direction
- It helps us focus our energy and attention
- We avoid wasting time, effort, money and energy on 'wrong' goals

Let's take each in turn.

Sense of direction

If we don't know exactly where we're going, how will we know whether we're on track or not, and whether we've arrived or not?

Referring back to the Principles for Success in Chapter 3 (p.37), if we:

- Know what we want

  AND

- Are aware enough to know whether or not we're on track

  AND

- Are able to be flexible to make changes if we're not on track

  THEN

We have a far better chance of achieving our desired outcome. So having clear goals will help give us a sense of direction and avoid us taking the wrong approach.

Focus our energy and attention

Having clear goals helps us to focus our energy and attention. Remembering back to the Communication Model and the amount of information that we have to filter out in order to function effectively, having goals helps us to focus on what is important to us. Within the mind is a function called 'the

Reticular Activation System', which acts like an internal radar, seeking out opportunities and situations that can help us achieve what we want. So by having clearly defined goals to focus on, we can pay attention to the things that will help us achieve them.

Avoid wasting time and effort on a 'wrong' goal

Some people realise en route to their goal (or even once they have achieved their goal) that what they thought they wanted is not what they really want. Using NLP goal-setting techniques, we consider the implications of achieving our goals when setting them and hence be able to set goals that are right for us, saving valuable time, effort, money and energy.

ACTION POINT

Make a list of three or more goals that you have. Feel free to do so in different areas of your life, such as work, health/fitness, education, relationships and money. We will come back to these at the end of the chapter.

TYPES OF GOALS

One of my particular areas of interest is sport, an area where setting goals is widely-used. There are three types of goals referred to in the sporting world:

- **Outcome goals**: These are the big picture goals such as 'winning the county marathon race', or in the workplace 'becoming a qualified lawyer' or 'getting my company to become a FTSE 250 company' (assuming I am the owner or managing director).

- **Performance goals**: These are the performance we would need to achieve to give us the best chance of achieving the outcome goal, for example 'running the marathon in less than three hours', or 'scoring 70% in my lawyer mock exams' or 'generating pre-tax profits of £100 million'. It is useful to set performance goals because sometimes there are factors outside our control, such as the performance of other runners or other companies, which can impact on the achievement of the outcome goal.

- **Process goals**: These are the specific tasks that would need to be done to achieve the performance goals. Examples could be 'running 10 miles in less than one hour, twice per week', or 'studying each main area of law for at least five hours per week' or 'winning three new customers a month and creating one new product each quarter'. Depending on the goal, the distinctions between performance and process goals can be blurred. Generally outcome goals are more compelling than performance and process goals, which can be seen as milestones along the way.

In NLP, the terms 'goals' and 'outcomes' are often used interchangeably.

HOW TO SET GOALS

In NLP there is a concept of having a Well-Formed Outcome. Well-formed outcomes are goals/outcomes that meet the Well-Formed Conditions for goals/outcomes, ie they are formed in such a way that it is more likely they will be achieved. Setting well-formed outcomes is extremely useful if we want to give ourselves the best chance of achieving our goals. That is not to say that people must follow the principles that will be outlined in this chapter in order to succeed, only that when they do follow these principles they improve their chances of success. Many people are aware of 'SMART' goals (Specific, Measurable, Achievable, Realistic, Timed) from their work appraisals; well-formed outcomes take SMART principles much further.

Let's take each of the well-formed conditions for goals/outcomes briefly in turn. At the end of this section, we will look at some examples of well-formed outcomes.

Stated in the positive

It is important to state goals in the positive so that we are focused on what it is that we actually want. One reason for this is because what we focus on increases in our mind, and it is more useful to have what we *do* want increase in our mind rather than what we *don't* want. If the goal is stated in negative terms or with some comparatives, then to some degree we are thinking about what we don't want. This could be one of the factors why some people find it difficult to stop smoking or eating certain foods. Saying 'I don't want to smoke or eat chocolate' is focusing on what the person doesn't want, and hence it keeps it in their mind.

Also, there are many directions in which we can move away from what we don't want, and relatively few directions to move towards what we do want. Knowing that 'I don't want to struggle when I retire' does not help me to have a goal to move towards when I retire. Wanting to have a specified annual income (for example £30,000 pa) does give me something to move towards. So state the goal in the positive, for example 'to have an income of £30,000 pa', or 'to have a net worth of £600,000 when I retire'.

Specific, measurable and undeniable

The more specific and measurable you can make the goal, the more you will know whether or not you're on target, and when you've achieved it. Make it so specific and measurable that you know what you will be

Say it how you want it to be!

TOP TIPS

seeing, hearing, saying to yourself and touching/feeling (and possibly smelling and tasting) when you achieve the goal. Make the goal so specific that you will know *undeniably* that you have achieved what you want.

Also, with certain goals, it is useful to be specific about where, when and with whom you want it, for example working for a charity within 15 miles of your (stated) home town.

TOP TIPS

Set goals that can be objectively measured, rather than goals around feelings such as 'feeling happy', 'feeling fit'. By all means include feelings in the goal, but please make sure that there are specifics. Normally having specifics will mean there are numbers and/or amounts.

Target date

Some goal-setting techniques do not cover this point. They either aren't specific with a date, or they say things like 'within six months', or 'on 15 July' (which year?). Be specific with the date and if necessary, the exact time of day.

🔍 EXAMPLE

A client of a colleague had something she wanted to achieve as a particular goal 'within three years'. Two years down the line she had hardly progressed. One of the first pieces of coaching my colleague gave her was to set a specific date, and she made more progress in the following three months than she had made in the previous two years.

One of my students on a course wanted to swim a certain distance by 30 June. He emailed me some time later to say that he had succeeded, but it was a year later than he wanted because he didn't write which year, demonstrating the point that it is best to be specific.

Also, in some situations it is useful to extend the date and slightly amend the goal initially thought of, so that we really know we have achieved what we want. For example, if someone wants to set up a business by 31 December 20XX, I would suggest that they set timed and specific goals that result from this, for example, to have been running a business for six months to 30 June 20XX (ie six months later) and to have sold a stated amount of money by that date and have a stated amount of orders in the pipeline. Starting one's own business probably isn't the real goal. Running a *successful* business probably is.

Under our influence

Where the achievement of a goal is under our influence, and we can initiate and maintain the progress towards achieving it, we are more likely to achieve it than if we have less influence or cannot initiate or maintain the progress. This does not mean that we have to do everything ourselves. In many situations, particularly at work, we need the co-operation or support of others to achieve our goals. Much of this book will have information about how to influence people to assist you.

Where organisations and teams achieve the goals/targets set by management, it is likely to be because managers are able to influence colleagues and staff to want to take steps towards achieving them. Achieving organisational goals/targets is a huge topic and outside the scope of this book, although we will provide some useful pointers, particularly in Chapters 8 (p.119) and 13 (p.181).

TOP TIPS

During a NLP goal-setting seminar one of my students mentioned a phrase he often used:

'If it's going to be, it's up to me'

How apt!

Ecological, responsible and right for you

We have already touched on the topic of ecology in Chapter 1 (p.9). This will be covered more fully a little later this chapter. At this juncture the key points are that the goals you set must be:

- Appropriate for you in *all* aspects of your life

- Appropriate and acceptable for those around you, with the (long-term) positive consequences far outweighing any possible (short-term) negative consequences (such as the time and effort involved). If this is the case, people in your life will probably be supportive of you in achieving the results you want

- In alignment with your sense of self, of who you really are

- Worth the time, effort, money and energy required to achieve it

The goal beyond the goal

I once heard John Grinder (one of the co-developers of NLP) say that, in his experience (which I assume is quite considerable), probably the single most important factor in people not achieving their desired goals is that they don't have a goal beyond the goal.

From an intuitive point of view this makes sense, because if there is nothing beyond the goal to strive for, the goal could lose its meaning and, at an extreme, could become almost pointless.

On the other side of the coin, a goal becomes even more motivating if, by achieving it, other possibilities become available or more doors are opened. (For example, gaining a degree will lead to greater career possibilities, and for some people the achievement of being able to run a marathon will lead to a greater sense of confidence in work and personal life.) If a goal becomes even more motivating it becomes more likely that we will do whatever it takes (within reason) to achieve that goal.

Realistic and achievable

At first glance this seems obvious. Of course a goal must be achievable and realistic for it to be achieved.

Yet in many walks of life, there have been exceptional feats and ground-breaking achievements such as the four-minute mile and climbing Mount Everest. Generally I find it useful to ask whether someone in a broadly similar situation to my client has done something similar. A 20 year old man who has recently run the 100 metres in 10 seconds has a reasonable chance of being able to run 9.9 seconds. A 90 year-old man who has never played sport is unlikely to be able to do so.

A couple of other relevant pointers related to realistic and achievable are:

TOP TIPS

Set goals which are challenging yet achievable.

• Is the first step specified and achievable? If not, it is a recipe for procrastination. According to an ancient proverb, 'A journey of a thousand miles begins with a single step.'

• Is there more than one way to achieve the goal? The more options, the better.

One final point on this topic. If by some chance you don't think the goal is achievable for you, yet someone in a similar situation to you would be able to achieve it, then it's worth asking yourself if you have some form of negative belief that means that others could do it but you can't. If you do identify a negative belief, you will find some pointers to changing beliefs later in this book. It may also be useful to see a qualified NLP Practitioner/Master Practitioner.

Resources

It is useful to consider what resources and skills would be needed to achieve the goal, and the extent to which we have them or could get them. Resources can be anything from specific tools (for example, the right textbooks when studying or a colour laser printer) through to more personal attributes such as confidence, the ability to concentrate or a sense of humour.

Acting 'as if' you had the resources, particularly the personal resources, may assist you in actually performing in a way you would like to. In Nightingale Conant's CD Series called *The Science of Personal Achievement* featuring Napoleon Hill, Hill mentions that he created a very successful publishing company in the 1930s with virtually no capital. Later he was told by other successful publishers that normally US$1 million of capital was required to do this. Hill remarked that because he didn't know that, he acted as if he could start a successful company with little capital. Believing you have the necessary resources can help you perform as if you do. Please use common sense here – acting as if you had a seat-belt on when doing rally-car driving is not appropriate!

As if now

According to Napoleon Hill, all of the successful business people he interviewed had a mental image of already having achieved the goal they wanted. This is also true for many sports champions, who see themselves having already won the event or trophy. In other words, they are stating (or at least thinking about) the goal in the 'now', as if it had already happened. This links back to 'specific, measurable and undeniable' where you imagine what will you be seeing, hearing, feeling etc when you have achieved the goal.

TOP TIPS

When setting goals, resist any temptation to use the phrases 'I want...' or 'I will be/have...' Say it in the present tense, as if it is happening or has happened. Remember, *say it how you want it to be.*

ECOLOGY AND GOALS

As you remember from Chapter 1 (p.9), ecology is the study of the consequences of our actions and behaviours on other parts of our life and on the lives of others. In order to ensure that we have a well-formed outcome and to give us the best chance of success, we need to fully consider the ecology (ie the consequences or impact) of achieving our goals. Here are some extremely valuable questions to assist you in doing this.

1. For what purpose do you want this?

2. What will you gain if you achieve this goal?

3. What will you lose if you achieve this goal?

4. What will happen if you achieve it?

5. What will happen if you don't achieve it?

6. What won't happen if you achieve it?

7. What won't happen if you don't achieve it? (A brain-twister, and a very useful question).

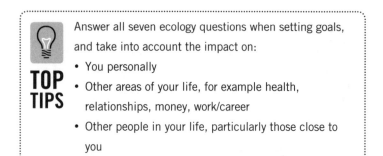

Answer all seven ecology questions when setting goals, and take into account the impact on:

• You personally
• Other areas of your life, for example health, relationships, money, work/career
• Other people in your life, particularly those close to you

Ideally, a goal is ecological if:

• There are ultimately no negative consequences of achieving the goal.

• Any short-term negative consequences are more than compensated for by positive ones. For example it may be worth the 'sacrifice' of not being able to socialise as much as you would like for the next year or two in order to obtain your Masters Degree or complete your exams to become a lawyer.

• The answers to all seven questions point to it being appropriate for you to achieve the goal.

Address any possible negative consequences with whoever will be affected *before* starting out towards the goal.

Q EXAMPLE

I met a couple at a wedding. He had been working around 16 hours per day 5–6 days per week for the previous 18 months on a project which would significantly help his career, plus they had a new baby (he obviously found some time to unwind!). They seemed to have a very good relationship. During the conversation they said that they recognised this would be a challenging period, and they had made agreements about how they would cope with the situation as a couple before he accepted the job, and then kept to those agreements. Because they had considered and planned for the consequences in advance, he was able to achieve a career goal whilst maintaining a strong relationship.

Practical pointers for goal setting

Remember the principles of outcome (big picture and/or long-term), performance (what you need to do) and process (how you will do it) goals, which link to long, medium and short-term goals respectively. When setting goals, set the outcome goal, plus some performance and/or process goals, rather like tasks or milestones along the way. The performance and/or process goals break the outcome goal down into more manageable chunks, making it seem less daunting.

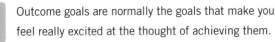

Outcome goals are normally the goals that make you feel really excited at the thought of achieving them.

TOP TIPS

EXAMPLES OF WELL-FORMED GOALS

Here are some examples of well-formed goals in different contexts. Please assume that the goals are ecological, achievable and meet the other well-formed conditions.

- It is 31 December 20XX and I weigh 70 kgs. I feel fit and healthy. (Remember to add this – it's possible to achieve the target weight but have the flu/be unwell – *say it how you want it to be!*)

- It is 31 May 20XX. I started my new business 12 months ago, and have sold £80,000 and made a pre-tax profit of £35,000. I have orders for the next eight months of £100,000.

- It is 31 August 20XX and I have swum the English Channel.

WHAT TO ASK YOURSELF WHEN SETTING GOALS

Here is a summary of the questions to ask yourself when setting goals. You could also use the information in this chapter to assist a colleague, friend or partner in setting goals.

1. Is the goal stated positively, with no negations or comparatives?

2. Is it specific and measurable? How will I know undeniably when I have achieved it? What will I be seeing, hearing, feeling, saying to myself and even smelling and tasting, when I have it? Where, when, how and with whom do I want it/not want it?

3 Is there a specified date/time?

4 Can I make it happen?   Can I start and maintain the achievement of the goal?

5 Is it ecological? Is it truly right for me, the people around me and society generally? Have I asked myself the seven ecology questions?

6 Will this outcome/goal increase my options and choices? What will this outcome get for me or allow me to do? How will it help me beyond the achievement of the goal?

7 Is the goal realistic and achievable? Have I ever had or done this before? Do I know anyone who has?

8. What resources are needed? What do I have now, and what do I need to get my outcome? Can I act as if I have it (if appropriate)?

9. Is the goal stated as if it has already happened?

 **ACTION POINT**

Re-visit the goals you set at the start of this chapter. Consider them in light of what you have read in this chapter, and re-write them and/or re-set them as appropriate.

There is anecdotal evidence that writing down your well-formed goals makes it more likely that you will achieve them.

TOP TIPS

QUICK RECAP

- Setting goals is an essential part of achieving what you want. It is one of the Principles for Success. By knowing what you want and setting goals appropriately, you are far more likely to achieve your goal and avoid wasting time striving for goals which are not right for you.

- Set different types of goals – outcome (big picture and/or long-term), performance (what you are going to do and/or medium-term) and process (how you are going to do it and/or short-term) goals, using the principles outlined in this chapter.

- Pay particular attention to whether the goal is ecological (ie right for you and the people around you), and whether by achieving it you will have more choice, options and subsequent benefits just from achieving this one goal.

- Set goals for each of the main areas of your life, such as career, family, health/fitness and finances, so that you can takes steps to have the kind of life you want.

- Review your goals regularly. Do they need tweaking or updating in the light of new circumstances?

- Once you have achieved your goal, set new goals when the time is right for you to do so.

PART 2

COMMUNICATION – LEARNING THE MANY SUBTLETIES

PART 2

CHAPTER 5

Getting people on your side: how to build trust with anyone

This chapter is primarily about how to create a feeling of trust and co-operation between yourself and other people. In NLP we call this building rapport. As you will remember from the Principles for Success discussed in Chapter 3, and creating well-formed outcomes (especially the section headed *Under our influence*) from Chapter 4, being able to get people on your side is an essential life skill.

Before we cover being able to build rapport effectively, there is one essential building block which is required. It is the ability to notice the impact of your communication on other people, and whether or not your communication is having the desired effect. In NLP this ability to notice or observe other people is called Sensory Acuity. Because sensory acuity is a building block for rapport, we briefly cover this first, then move on to techniques for building rapport.

WHY IS SENSORY ACUITY SO USEFUL?

People communicate all the time, both verbally and non-verbally. In fact, as we will see later in this chapter, much of our communication is non-verbal.

The ability to 'pick up on' people's communication, some of which can be very subtle and unknown even to the other person, can give us clues about how to proceed during meetings and conversations. This skill is something that most people can do easily with people they know well. Many of us will see someone we know well and immediately know that they are happy or not happy, without them saying anything. Equally, if we hear the way they say 'Hello', we can often tell the mood they are in. To be able to use these observational skills not just with people we know well, but also with, for example, acquaintances, new clients or prospects and new students, will help us to influence and communicate more effectively. It will help us know whether what we are saying and the way we are saying it is having the desired impact. If it is not having the impact we would like, it would probably make sense to change the way we are communicating. This links back to the Principles for Success – have an outcome in mind (in this case, the message we want to send), use our awareness (sensory acuity) to gather information and be flexible if the message is not having the desired effect.

WHAT ARE THE SIGNS TO BE AWARE OF?

When observing other people, there are several non-verbal signs to pay attention to which could indicate how someone is feeling, for example:

- Breathing patterns (fast/slow, chest or abdomen)
- Pupil size

- Eye focus

- Fullness of the lower lip

- Skin colour (light or dark for that person)

- Clusters of gestures (such as hand movements, foot tapping, body posture)

- Voice tonality (volume, speed, intonation)

- Facial muscle movements

If someone lets you know they are feeling a particular way (for example excited, motivated, angry) and you make a mental note of the outward signs (in NLP, we call this Calibrating), if you see these signs again you will have a pretty good idea of how they are feeling. This is what you do automatically when you know how people you know well are feeling.

CAVEATS

It is important to note that, when you are calibrating, you are comparing one person to him/herself, not to other people. For example, when Fred's skin colour gets darker and there are more lines on his forehead, it could mean that he is angry, whereas when George displays the *same* signs it could mean that he is confused or something else other than angry.

Some people naturally show their emotions more than others, and hence are more easy to calibrate.

TOP TIPS

Avoid jumping to conclusions based on non-verbal signals, particularly if you don't know the person well. Check out your assumptions. And of course, use common sense – someone shouting abuse is almost certainly angry, and may be best left alone.

ACTION POINT

When you see someone you will see again (such as a colleague, partner, client, or friend) in a distinct state (such as happy, sad, angry, confused, excited, motivated), calibrate his/her outward signs. Remember these signs when you next see/hear them in that person. As you become more adept, choose other people and practise. It may be prudent not to tell them what you are doing!

BUILDING RAPPORT

Rapport is one of the Principles for Success, and can be defined as creating a spirit of trust and respect between people so that they are more likely to co-operate with you.

Why is rapport so important?

Many of us are able to unknowingly build rapport with friends and partners. Being able to build and maintain rapport is essential to any good relationship, be it personal or professional, such as when selling, recruiting, doing appraisals, wanting your teenage children to open up to you, teaching – it's difficult to think of situations where rapport would *not* be useful!

Rapport is not the same as agreeing with someone. In fact, it is completely appropriate and possible to maintain rapport even when disagreeing. By doing so, it maintains the mutual trust even if there is disagreement. You can probably think of times when someone disagreed with you yet felt that you trusted them, and also times when someone agreed with you and yet didn't feel you could trust them.

Sometimes as a boss or parent we need to challenge our colleagues or children. Medical professionals may need to give bad news to patients or deal with upset relatives. If we have this underlying trust and rapport, others will be far more likely to co-operate with us or hear what we are saying than if there is a lack of rapport.

Another indicator of why learning about rapport is so useful is that it is taught on many sales courses. I attended a one day sales course at the Institute of Directors in 2001, and the trainer spent around 1–2 hours talking about and teaching rapport and related skills. If it's seen as a key skill in a totally results oriented environment such as selling, it is obviously a useful skill to have.

Q EXAMPLE

After I set up my coaching business in 1999, I still worked 4–6 days per month as a part-time finance director whilst I was studying NLP and building up my business. I had a meeting with a software company, which was looking for a finance director one day per week.

There were three directors. I met the first two, and everything was fine. Then I met the managing director, and although he was a really nice guy, for some reason the meeting wasn't going well. And I couldn't figure out why (have you ever had that feeling?).

Then I remembered what I had just learned during my NLP Practitioner course about rapport, and started to put it into practice. Literally within moments, the whole atmosphere changed, we became very engaged with each other. The meeting flowed, I got the assignment, and it went so well that he asked me to be his personal coach after he sold the business several months later.

The following sections will outline how I turned the meeting around.

Some background information

There are two key principles of building rapport. The first is that people tend to like people who are like them. Secondly, the majority of communication is non-verbal. There have been studies which show that in face to face communication:

- 55% of communication is based on body language
- 38% is based on voice tonality
- Only 7% is based on the words we say

This means that up to 93% of communication is non-verbal and out of our conscious awareness. Whether these figures are 'correct' is not the issue. We have all experienced a gesture or look (body language) from parents, bosses, colleagues or partners which means everything is fine, and another which means things are absolutely not fine. As a child I can remember teachers saying my name (just one word) in a certain tone and I knew things were fine, and in another tone and I knew I was in trouble!

Equally we may have been in situations where a colleague, client or team-mate says something and we just have a 'gut feeling' they are not being totally honest. And as for watching and listening to some politicians... If the words and the voice and/or body language are giving mixed or contradictory messages, we will tend to believe the non-verbal signals.

How can we build and maintain rapport?

So the question is, how can we use non-verbal communication to demonstrate that we are like someone and hence build rapport?

The answer is to Match or Mirror aspects of their body language and/or voice tonality. For example, if someone had their right hand on their hip, you would be matching their posture if you had your right hand on your hip, and you would be mirroring if you faced them and had your left hand on your hip.

What aspects of body language and voice tonality can we match?

There are several aspects, and we will cover those that are more obvious and easy to use.

TOP TIPS

Please note when reading the following that matching or mirroring is best done subtly and outside of the other person's conscious awareness.

Body language (55%)

We can match the following:

- Gestures: such as nodding or hand movements

- Posture: such as folding arms, crossing legs, leaning forward or back or to one side

- Breathing: such as how fast someone is breathing

It is appropriate to match certain aspects of someone's **posture** when they are talking – and remember, please do it subtly. However, please only match someone's **gestures** when it is *your* turn to talk. Matching someone's arm-waving while *they* are talking will really annoy them and break rapport.

Matching breathing is particularly useful when there are silences. As a coach I sometimes ask challenging questions of my clients, and match their breathing as they reflect.

Voice tonality (38%)

We can match the following:

- Speed of speech: fast or slow

- Volume of speech: loud or quiet

- Pitch or tone of speech: high or low

We can also use words (7%) to build rapport – this will be covered in Chapters 6 (p.81) and 7 (p.93).

Cross-Over Mirroring

Occasionally it may not be appropriate or possible to directly match/mirror. For example, would a woman match a man who was sitting with his legs open and his hands folded across his chest around his pectoral muscles? Probably not. In such situations one thing you can do to match physiology is to do 'cross-over mirroring', which is mirroring/matching a part of someone's physiology with a different part of yours. So in the example above, the woman might cross her legs and leave her arms slightly wider apart.

The woman could still match his voice, and as we will see in the next couple of chapters, she could also match using words.

Building rapport with more than one person

There may be situations where we want to build rapport with more than one person at a time, for example panel interviews and meetings. We can match one aspect of one person's physiology and other parts of someone else, and use our voice and words to build rapport with several people. Or, once we have rapport with one person, we can switch to match other people, occasionally returning to matching the people we have previously matched and built rapport with.

Pacing and Leading

In NLP we call matching someone's body language or voice tonality for a period of time, Pacing. This period of time can range from a few seconds to several minutes, possibly even longer depending on circumstances. One very useful way for us to know whether we have built rapport is to slowly/gently/subtly change aspects of our body language and/or voice tonality and notice whether the other person follows. This is called Leading. If the person you are communicating with follows your lead automatically you probably have a good level of rapport. If the person does not follow your lead go back to matching again, observing more attentively (pacing, and using your sensory acuity skills) before leading again.

TOP TIPS

Here are some tips to build and maintain rapport:

- Pick one or two aspects to match. Attempting to match everything will probably overwhelm you, and even if you do it, the other person will probably spot it.

- Be subtle. For example, if someone crosses their arms, wait a few moments before crossing yours rather than doing so immediately.

- A little goes a long way. You don't have to completely match the full extent of someone's gestures, posture or voice tonality. For example, if someone makes large hand movements with both hands when they speak, when it's your turn to speak you can use smaller similar hand movements with one or both hands.The same applies when matching voice. For example, if someone speaks loudly, and you normally speak quietly, increase your volume somewhat.

- If things are going well in a meeting and you both feel comfortable, assume that you are in rapport. If you don't feel comfortable, the chances are that the other person won't feel comfortable, and hence it may be useful to use some of the rapport-building techniques

- Be patient. Pace the other person by, for example, speaking closer to their pace or volume than you normally would, and then when you feel in rapport adjust the pace or volume to one that is more comfortable. If the person follows, that is an excellent indicator that you are in rapport. In NLP the suggested pace:lead ratio is roughly 3:1.

- Even when disagreeing with someone, or delivering a potentially difficult message (for example giving some feedback about inadequate performance), if it is appropriate to stay in rapport (which it probably will be), stay in rapport. Even though the message may be unpleasant for the other person to receive, there will be an underlying sense of trust if you stay in rapport.

- If someone is agitated and you want to calm the situation (for example, if you are work in customer services), match their energy levels (for example loud voice, fast speech) with 'non-confrontational' language.

- Use your common sense.

Remember, NLP has a powerful set of tools, which are best used to create win-win situations. If you use them to manipulate, people will realise it. Rapport is a particularly powerful tool – use it wisely.

ACTION POINT

Observe friends and partners in conversation in restaurants, cafes or bars. Notice how they automatically seem to match each other. Friends will reach for a glass of wine at similar times or lean forwards or back at the same time.

🔍 EXAMPLE

Returning to my story about the interview at the software company:

I noticed that the MD was leaning forward in his chair, and I was leaning back. We were completely mis-matching, completely out of rapport. I remembered that my NLP trainer had said 'a little goes a long way', and so I leant forward about half-way, and turned slightly towards him. After about 10–20 seconds, he leaned back further, turned towards me, and we were matching. From that point the meeting just 'felt' more comfortable, and progressed smoothly.

QUICK RECAP

- *A significant amount of communication is done non-verbally, via physiology and voice tonality.*
- *The ability to notice subtle changes in people's physiology and voice tonality is called Sensory Acuity.*
- *When Calibrating, you are comparing one person to themself, not to others.*
- *Practise developing your Sensory Acuity skills. It will help you build Rapport with people.*
- *Being able to build Rapport with people is essential to any good relationship.*
- *Build Rapport with people by Matching or Mirroring their body language (especially posture, gestures and breathing) and/or voice tonality (especially volume and speed of speech) for a period of time (Pacing). Do so subtly, out of conscious awareness. If you make it too obvious, people will know you have been reading about NLP! Remember, a little goes a long way.*

CHAPTER 6

How to speak everyone's language: becoming quad-lingual

Did you know that there are four languages within the English language? In this chapter, we will show you how to speak these four languages, which will mean that you will be able to communicate with just about anyone in the way they prefer to receive information. This chapter will help you get to grips with Representational Systems (visual, auditory, kinaesthetic, olfactory and gustatory) and use language so that you communicate with people the way they prefer.

WHY IS THIS IMPORTANT?

By having an awareness of the importance of our senses we can become better communicators, see eye to eye and get on the same wavelength as other people, get to grips with improving existing skills and learning new ones, teach/present information in a more palatable way for audiences and improve consultancy and problem solving skills at work.

In order to do this, it will be helpful to put another building block in place – our 'senses'.

HOW WE GATHER AND PROCESS INFORMATION

You will remember from the Communication Model that we use our five senses to take in external 'events' and then re-process them internally. These senses are:

- Seeing (visual)
- Hearing (auditory)
- Feeling (kinaesthetic)
- Smell (olfactory)
- Taste (gustatory)

In NLP we call these senses our Representational Systems. There is an additional representational system that we refer to in NLP, called Auditory Digital. This is our 'self-talk', our internal commentary on what we are seeing, hearing, feeling, tasting and smelling.

Our representational systems

We use all our representational systems to take in information from the outside world, and to process it internally. Although some people are equally comfortable using each of the representational systems, most of us will have a preference for using one or two of these senses over the others. Generally the olfactory and gustatory senses, important as they are for survival and basic needs, are not normally one of the preferences in Western culture. Let's briefly consider the three main representational systems (seeing, hearing and feeling) plus auditory digital.

Visual
This consists of taking external images, as well as creating images and visualising in our mind and also remembering pictures/ images we have seen. There are various professions where the visual system is used to a significant degree, such as designers, artists, photographers and architects.

Auditory
This consists of taking external sounds, as well as creating sounds in our mind and also remembering sounds/music/words we have heard. There are various professions where the auditory system is used to a significant degree, such as musicians, chat-show hosts and those doing a lot of work on the telephone.

Kinaesthetic
This is made up of external touch, internal sensations and emo-tions, as well as bodily awareness. There are various professions where the kinaesthetic system is used to a significant degree, such as athletics, nursing, massage and counselling.

Auditory Digital
This is our internal dialogue and assessment about whether something makes sense. Accountants, lawyers, financial analysts and bankers tend to use the auditory digital system significantly.

Preferred representational systems

Earlier we mentioned that people tend to prefer one or two of the representational systems over the others. We can think of our representational systems preferences like a recipe for a cake with four spices (ie the four main representational systems). Because people have different taste in cakes, they will like cakes made with a certain combination of the spices which suits their taste.

If we can be aware of someone's preferred representational system (ie their preferred recipe), we can present information to them according to *their* taste (which may be different from *our* taste). This is particularly relevant for professions where presenting information is important, such as teachers, trainers, presenters, managers and salespeople.

In addition to being aware of other peoples' representational systems, it can be extremely useful for us to be aware of our own preferences and to become more flexible at using those representational systems that we are less accustomed to using. Going back to the recipe analogy, if we vary the amount of each spice we use, we can expand our experiences and flexibility of taste-buds. This awareness can help us to think about situations in a richer, more creative way.

Recognising people's preferred representational system

Here are some indications of how to spot people's Preferred representational systems. I would like to make clear that this section has some generalisations which may not be 'true' for every single person.

People whose preferred representational system is visual, ie prefer to think in pictures, tend to:

- Speak fast (they think in pictures, and a picture paints a thousand words)

- Use visual language such as *see, look, appear, focus, paint a picture, mental image, clear, in view of, hazy*

- Have hobbies and do work that involves seeing things, such as art, watching films, photography, or they like the visual aspect of their pasttimes, such as looking at scenery when walking in the country

- Remember things better when they have seen diagrams or flowcharts

- Like things to be neat and tidy; the way something looks is important

People whose preferred representational system is auditory, ie prefer to communicate using words, tend to:

- Speak at a medium pace, often in a rhythmic or melodious way

- Use auditory language such as *hear, sound, listen, speak, discuss, tune in/tune out, resonate, I'm all ears, voice an opinion*

- Have hobbies and do work that involves hearing or words, such as reciting poetry, listening to music, speaking to their friends on the phone, or they like the auditory aspect of their pastimes, such as hearing the sounds of nature when walking in the country

- Remember things better when they have discussed them

People whose preferred representational system is kinaesthetic, ie prefer to feel/experience things, tend to:

- Speak at a slow pace, because it takes time to process feelings

- Use kinaesthetic language such as *solid, grasp, make contact, kick some ideas around, hard, get hold of, get in touch with, catch onto*

- Have hobbies and do work that involves touching or emotions, such as physiotherapy, pottery, sports, counselling, or they like the kinaesthetic aspect of their pastimes, such as feeling the fresh air when walking in the country (walking is a kinaesthetic activity anyway)

- Remember things better when they have experienced them

People whose preferred representational system is auditory digital, ie prefer to think in ideas and to analyse, tend to:

- Want to *understand* how ideas work

- Be interested in ideas that *make sense and are logical*

- Use language that is not sensory specific, such as *conceive, think, understand, know, learn, process, decide, consider, change*

Using this information

When I run my NLP and communication training courses I ask delegates to complete a questionnaire similar to that in Appendix A (p.227). The preferences will vary depending on the type of audience, and are on average:

Rep System	Visual	Auditory/Auditory Digital	Kinaesthetic
%	35% – 40%	20% – 25%	40%

This information emphasises how important it is to be flexible in the way you communicate. For example, if you communicate kinaesthetically with a prospective client or student whose preferred system is visual, he/she may simply not be as engaged as if you communicated in a more visual way.

TOP TIPS

Use all of the four main representational systems when presenting ideas and concepts, and when teaching or training others. Pay particular attention as follows:

- When presenting to someone whose preferred system is visual, show them pictures, diagrams and flow charts. Make sure they are neat!
- When presenting to someone whose preferred system is auditory, talk to them about your ideas and enter into a discussion.
- When presenting to someone whose preferred system is kinaesthetic, let them have a hands-on experience or engage with them so they feel involved.
- When presenting to someone whose preferred system is auditory digital, make sure you have the logical, rational arguments to support your thoughts and ideas.

When presenting to groups of people, for example sales presentations, panel interviews, team meetings (as a manager or sports coach), doing marketing or advertising campaigns, incorporate all of the main representative systems.

ACTION POINT

Do the questionnaire in Appendix A (p.227). If you are a manager, consider asking your team to do it and sharing the answers with the rest of the team members, as a way of highlighting that we are all different.

Please remember that just because someone scores highly on, for example, auditory, that does not mean they are an auditory person, nor does it mean they are 'good' at listening or 'bad' at the other representational systems. The scores only show a preference at the time they are doing the questionnaire, not their competence.

I mentioned earlier that this knowledge can be used as a way to improve communication in teams, and hence have creative problem-solving. Here is an example.

Q EXAMPLE

One of my former business partners was asked to do some business process improvement for an organisation that had been employing teams of consultants trying to do this for several weeks.

He held a two–hour meeting/workshop for all the staff directly involved with the business process concerned. During that meeting he laid out several pieces of paper, representing all the different departments involved with the particular business process, on a big table so that everyone could see what was happening. Then, he asked people to discuss/talk about how the process worked, and how it could be improved (so that everyone could hear about the process and talk about the logic/rationale). During this process he used small objects (representing the flow of information) that attendees could move from department to department during the discussion – these objects had paper attached so that attendees could write on them. This helped people to have a kinaesthetic experience (hands on, moving things and writing).

By fully engaging the senses of all attendees people were more creative, and according to my partner they made more progress in two hours than they had done in weeks.

BECOMING QUAD-LINGUAL

In the section headed *Recognising people's preferred representational system*, one of the aspects to pay attention to is language. In NLP the words that denote which representational system someone is using are called Predicates; for example 'see' is a visual predicate. We tend to use predicates that reflect our preferred representational system, or at least the representational system we are thinking in at the time. Virginia Satir found in her family therapy that when people had a strong preference for a particular system, they would almost be speaking a different language to other family members when they were arguing, or explaining how they saw the situation (visual), or felt about it (kinaesthetic), or perceived it (auditory digital) or how the situation resonated with them (auditory). One way for us to use words to build rapport is by matching someone's predicates. And if we take the work-related example below we can see how it is possible to say almost the same thing in four different 'languages'.

Visual

'If I could *show* you an *attractive* way in which you could have XXX (potential benefits or values), you would at least want to *look* at it, wouldn't you? If this *looks good* to you we will go ahead and *focus* on getting the paperwork in.'

Auditory

'If I could *tell* you an attractive way in which you could have XXX (potential benefits or values), you would at least want to *hear* about it, wouldn't you? If this *sounds good* to you we will go ahead and *discuss* how to set up an account.'

Kinaesthetic

'If I could help you *get a hold of* a *concrete* way in which you could have XXX (potential benefits or values), you would at least want to *get a feel for it*, wouldn't you? If this *feels good* to you we will go ahead and *get to grips with* how to set up an account by *handling the paperwork.*'

Auditory Digital

'If I could *arrange* for you to *obtain* XXX (potential benefits or values), you would at least want to *estimate* its impact, wouldn't you? If this *makes sense* to you we will *proceed* and *consider* the way forward regarding the *requirements* for opening an account.'

(Please note that the italics emphasise the predicates to you, the reader. It is not necessary to stress them during the conversation or to italicise them in writing.)

TOP TIPS

- When presenting to certain professional groups, you may want to lean towards one of the representational systems, depending on the profession. For example, it is probably safe to assume that a group of musicians will have a well-developed auditory system, and that accountants/lawyers want things to be logical and make sense.
- Use predicates from all representational systems when speaking or writing to a group or people who you do not know.

ACTION POINT

Practise listening out for predicates. If you want to break it down into bite-size chunks, decide which representational system you will be practising on a specific day and then listen out for predicates from that system. You could also use mainly predicates from that system and then pick a different system the next day. Within a week or two you will become far more fluent in all four languages.

EYE PATTERNS

One other indicator of how someone is thinking is where their eyes look. Based on research and simple observation, the direction of someone's eye movements indicate which representational system they are accessing at any given moment. The diagram below shows the eye patterns for the vast majority of people, shown as you look at them.

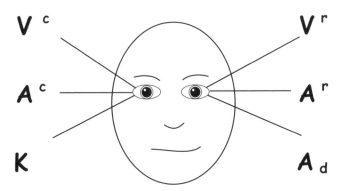

- Vc is Visual Construct, ie creating a picture of something you haven't seen.

- Vr is Visual Remembered, ie remembering a picture of something you have seen.

- Ac is Auditory Construct, ie creating a sound of something or words you haven't heard.

- Ar is Auditory Remembered, ie remembering a sound of something or of words you have heard.

- Ad is Auditory Digital, ie talking to yourself, or saying something in your own voice.

- K is Kinaesthetic, ie getting in touch with feelings or emotions.

It is important to note that there are some NLP professionals who have found that a small percentage of people can be 'reverse organised', whereby the items shown on the right hand side are on the left side and vice versa.

TOP TIPS

If you see someone's eyes go to a particular quadrant when thinking about a question or when speaking, it is an indication that they are accessing that particular representational system. Use the relevant predicates when speaking to them. For example, if you see someone's eyes go into visual construct, you could say, 'how does that look?', 'what would that look like?' or 'does that look OK?'

Please use common sense with this. Someone looking up may not be accessing visual – they might simply have seen a cobweb on the ceiling.

QUICK RECAP

- *There are five representational systems (visual, auditory, Kinaesthetic, Olfactory and Gustatory) plus Auditory Digital.*
- *Remember that we use all of the Representational Systems, and that many of us have a preferred system.*
- *We can use our knowledge of Representational Systems and Predicates to build Rapport and communicate more effectively with individuals and groups.*
- *There are various indicators of the preferred Representational System that someone has, such as how quickly they speak, the words they use, or the hobbies or work they choose.*
- *The more flexible we can be with using different Predicates the more we will speak the four different languages in English.*
- *Watching peoples' eye patterns can give us an indication of which Representational System someone is using at a given moment.*

CHAPTER 7

Using language to influence: choosing your words for maximum impact

This chapter continues the theme of language and the hidden power of words and questions. We will look at how it can be used to build rapport and communicate ideas even more effectively:

- How to use and change the degree of detail when communicating. At times abstract/big picture thinking is useful, and at other times getting into the detail is useful.
- How to think laterally.
- How to ask questions which can uncover missing information and hence shed useful light on situations.
- A few words about stories, metaphors and analogies.

WHY LEARN ABOUT LANGUAGE?

There are numerous ways, and areas of life, in which you could benefit from being able to use the ideas in this chapter:

- Selling, whether it be products and services in business, or concepts and ideas in management in the private or public sector
- Writing reports
- Marketing/advertising
- Coaching, either in sports or for life/business coaching
- Teaching/training, so that students/delegates gain the most from your input
- Creating mission statements
- Negotiations
- Planning projects
- Creative thinking
- Asking questions that save time and help get to the nub of issues
- Improving your career prospects

And remember, language is one of the key filters within the Communication Model, so the way we use language to communicate ideas, both to ourselves and others, can impact the meaning.

Let's consider the first main topic, which is called the Hierarchy of Ideas.

THE HIERARCHY OF IDEAS

At the two ends of the spectrum ideas can be either abstract/big picture or specific/detail. The Hierarchy of Ideas is a model of language that helps us to move our and other people's thinking from the abstract to the specific and vice versa if it would be useful, and even to think laterally and creatively.

Abstract ideas and concepts are ideas that you can't actually see, hear, feel, taste, or smell. Examples could be concepts such as *fulfilment, agreement, world peace, a fair taxation system, profitability* and *efficiency*. Specific ideas are things that are more physical and concrete, for example the details of *who, what, where, when* and *how*. Agreement is normally easier to attain when talking about abstract concepts. The desirability of attaining *world peace* is probably something we can all agree on. Agreeing *how* to do it is more difficult.

Why might we want to move the conversation or the thinking into abstract? Here are some possible reasons:

- To gain agreement at work or as a starting point for negotiations

- To develop a mission statement for a department or organisation.

- To agree the purpose of a meeting, so that it stays on track and the attendees do not go off at a tangent or get swamped by details.

- To gain an overview of situations.

- To help build rapport with people who prefer to think in big picture rather than detail.

We might want to get more details in order to:

- Plan projects

- Finalise agreements (dot the 'i's and cross the 't's).

- Understand what people mean by abstract words (what does a 'fair taxation system' mean? Fair to whom? According to whom? Compared to what?)

- Fix problems

- Help build rapport with people who prefer to think in detail rather than big picture.

One place where we can often observe the Hierarchy of Ideas in action is during media interviews with political leaders. The politicians want to speak about abstract concepts, partly because they know that most people will agree on the desirability of concepts such as 'a fair taxation system', 'opportunities for everyone', and 'economic stability'. Interviewers want to know how specifically the politicians will achieve these concepts, and endeavour to ask for details, and politicians are frequently reluctant to provide such details.

By way of terminology, in NLP we refer to becoming more abstract as Chunking up (ie upwards) and getting into more details as Chunking down (ie downwards).

Becoming more abstract

Let's consider a simple example of becoming more abstract, and then we'll look at a more practical example in a work environment. Initially let's consider 'cars'. If we want to get more abstract (chunk up) regarding cars, we could ask questions such as:

- What is the purpose of cars?

- What do cars do for us?

- What is your intention of having a car?

- What is car an example of?

Answers could include, 'to get to places quicker', 'to help us be comfortable', 'to help us be safe', 'to make us feel proud' or 'a mode of transport', depending on the question asked. In each case (comfort, speed, safety, pride and transportation) the answer is more abstract than 'car'; a car is one of many ways for people to have any of the five benefits mentioned. Also, the answers are fairly abstract – it's difficult to actually see, for example, 'pride' or 'comfort'. We can chunk up further on any of the answers, which might lead us from *'fast transport'* to *'save time and do more'* to *'have more fun'* to *'be more fulfilled'*, each being a higher level of abstraction than the previous.

🔍 EXAMPLE

I was asked to help an international organisation create a mission statement. Mission statement is clearly an abstract concept. Due to the nature of the organisation and its product, many of the senior people had an excellent technical knowledge of the product. Because they had been so used to thinking about the product (ie detail), they struggled to see the big picture of what they were doing. However, by persevering with the chunking up questions, they were able to arrive at a mission statement that motivated all the team and truly summarised what the organisation stood for.

Becoming more detailed

If we want to get more specific (chunk down) about 'cars', we can sub-divide cars into at least two aspects – makes of car and parts of the car. We can ask questions about *who, what, where, when* and *how*, and it is often useful to add the words specifically or exactly too. For example, 'which make of car, specifically?', 'which part of the car is broken?', 'exactly how old is the car?', 'when exactly did you buy the car?', 'who owned it before you?', 'how many miles has it done?' and 'where do you have it serviced?'. As you have probably realised, there are more questions to gain greater detail than to gain greater abstraction. Also, we can ask additional chunking down questions in response to the answers, to get even deeper level of detail if that would be useful.

A work-based example

Imagine that a team of managers is discussing whether to have a new computer system. Both chunking up and chunking down can be useful in the discussion. Asking, *'what's the benefit/purpose of having the new system?'*, and considering whether that benefit is in line with the organisation's goals, are probably useful questions to ask before making the decisions to commission a new system and which system to choose.

Once the big picture has been agreed, it will then probably be useful to get into the detail of who does what by when, what is the specification of the new system so that it will meet the benefits previously identified, the precise spending limits etc. To delve into the detail without having considered the big picture may be a waste of time, and may not meet the key benefits identified by the chunking up questions. Not to get into the details could mean that the implementation or selection of the system is not as effective as it could be.

Q EXAMPLE

In the early 1990s (before I knew about NLP) I was on the Education Committee for a fairly small professional body. I had missed several of the monthly meetings for various reasons, and when I attended the next meeting the committee was discussing the detail of how it was going to revamp the teaching manuals and other educational material, at a cost of around £250,000 (a significant sum for the organisation). It had done a major update 18 months previously. When it came to my turn to speak, at the risk of going over ground I had missed, I asked for an explanation of the purpose of spending this amount of money revamping something that had been fairly recently updated. There was silence, and no one could provide a compelling answer. After the meeting the chairman of the committee phoned me to thank me for the question, and told me that they had decided to keep the existing materials.

TOP TIPS

Develop the ability to see the big picture *and* do detail. Generally, people who rise to the top of an organisation need to be able to see the big picture, as well as get into the detail if there are problems. In sport, coaches who can both be aware of the technical aspects of the sport (detail) and see the big picture tactically will be more likely to become the head coach/team manager.

Summary of the Hierarchy of Ideas

The following table summarises the Hierarchy of Ideas.

Level	Some useful questions	Example 1
Big picture/ abstract (Potential areas of Agreement)	• What is the purpose of X? • What will X do for you? • What is your intention by doing X? • What is X an example of?	Fulfilling life ↑ More fun ↑ Save time, do more ↑ Fast transport ↑ **Car**
Detail/specific (Potential areas of Disagreement)	• What are examples of this? • Who/what/when/where/how specifically? • How do you know specifically?	Make → Brand X → Model Y Part → Engine → Pistons

ACTION POINT

Practise chunking up and chunking down. Pick an idea that you are working on, and ask the relevant Chunking up questions to get the big picture. Equally, ask yourself detailed questions to uncover more information. **Please** only do this with a purpose in mind – we could get overwhelmed by gathering too much detail. Notice for yourself which end of the spectrum you feel more comfortable with, and practise the other if that would be useful for you.

Lateral thinking

The Hierarchy of Ideas can also be used as a structure to help 'lateral thinking', which can be particularly useful for creative thinking and brainstorming. (**NB** lateral thinking is 'a way of solving problems by employing unorthodox and seemingly illogical means'.)

Lateral chunking is a two step process. Step 1 is to chunk up for a bigger picture, and then step 2 is to chunk down, asking for a different example (of the bigger picture).

For example, chunking up from '*car*' we could get '*transport*', and when asked for a different example of '*transport*' someone could say '*lorry*'. Equally, the benefit of '*cars*' could be '*excitement*', and another example of something that gives '*excitement*' could be anything from '*watching a spy film*' to '*bungee jumping*'.

UNCOVERING WHAT PEOPLE MEAN

The principles of the Hierarchy of Ideas can be used as a guide to using language. In this section we will be covering how to become more specific as a way to gain more information about what people mean, which has several benefits as you will see.

Overview

As you remember from the Communication Model in Chapter 2 (p.19) we *delete*, *distort* and *generalise* in our mind. Given that the words we use are *a* reflection (not *the* reflection) of what is in our mind, our language contains deletions, distortions and generalisations.

In Chapter 2 we also saw that these three ways of filtering are not good or bad; they are simply what people do, and sometimes we filter in ways that are useful, and other times in ways that are not useful. This can also be reflected in our language.

In this section, we will cover how to recognise the presence of these filters from the words people use, and how to use questions to uncover facts that might reveal useful information. There are several possible benefits of being able to do this, including:

• Saving time and helping get to the heart of the matter quickly

• Gaining clarity on what people mean and avoiding misunder-standings

• Identifying blocks in people's thinking

• Gaining access to relevant information to be able to make better decisions

By way of example, if several attendees of a meeting were asked for their thoughts it's possible that we could hear some of the following replies:

1. *'They are planning something'*

2. *'The communication in this place is interesting'*

3. *'We never get told anything'* or *'we always get told everything'*

4. *'I know my boss has some unusual ideas about me'*

5. *'Their not answering us means changes will happen'*

Most of the statements could be interpreted in a wide variety of ways. As the reader, do you really know what is meant by any of these five sentences above? In these statements, a lot of information has been:

- Distorted (replies 4 and 5 could be countered with *'how do you know your boss has unusual ideas about you?'*, and *'how does their not answering you mean changes will happen?'*)

- Generalised (reply 3 could be countered with *'never? anything? always? everything?'*)

- Deleted (replies 1 and 2 could be countered with *'who specifically are "they"?'*, *'which place?'*, *'what are "they" planning?'*, *'in what way is it interesting?'*, *'what is being communicated?'*)

We will look more closely at some indicators, or language patterns, for each of the three main filters – distortion, generalisation and deletion. For each of the three filter types we will cover:

- What the pattern is

- How it works

- How to ask relevant questions to uncover what has been distorted, generalised or deleted if it is appropriate to do so

The questions to uncover more information about distortions, generalisations and deletions are known in NLP as The Meta Model. This model was developed by Grinder and Bandler from their modelling of Virginia Satir, who used these types of questions in her therapy work to uncover what her clients actually meant and how they arrived at some of their unhelpful conclusions about the meaning of various events and behaviours.

Please note that with the following examples, especially the 'challenges' or probing questions to the language patterns, it is *essential* to use common sense, have a purpose for asking the questions and be in rapport.

The language of distortion

Distortions are when someone considers or experiences an event and interprets it in some way that makes it mean something that it may not mean. This can also lead to people jumping to conclusions. There are four main patterns to consider:

1. Mind reads

2. Causations

3. Equivalences

4. Anonymous judgements

Mind reads

Mind reads are where we claim to know what someone is thinking or feeling, which may or may not be correct. For example, 'I know you're wondering why I called this meeting' could have the effect of making people think or feel how *you* assume they think or feel – in other words, putting ideas into people's heads.

Indications of mind reads are plausible sentences starting with phrases like those in bold below:

- '**I know you're wondering** how quickly we can beat last year's figures.'

- '**I'm sure you want** to show the crowd just how great you are.'

- '**I can tell you want** to enjoy yourself tonight.'

- '**You probably already know** that we're the fastest growing software company in London.'

Sometimes people use mind reads in ways which limit them. You can probe for more information about the mind read by asking, 'How do you know (specifically) that ....?' (ie what is your evidence procedure?) For example:

- '**I know** she doesn't like me.'

Probe with: 'How specifically do you know she doesn't like you?'

- '**I know** you don't want to be here.'

  Probe with: 'How do you know we don't want to be here?'

- '**I know** they are all afraid of me.'

  Probe with: How do you know they are afraid of you?'

Notice in these three examples we want to check out how specifically they know (or what their evidence is). We would probably *not* want to ask questions like, 'why doesn't she like you?', which would be agreeing with their potentially distorted opinion in this instance.

Causations

Causations are where someone states/proposes that something *causes* or *leads* to something else, which may be true for them and is almost certainly *not* the only possible interpretation of the event or situation.

We can create causations as follows. The key 'causative' words are shown in bold:

- '**Because** you're making lots of sales calls, you will become even better at handling objections.'

- '**If you** eat all your greens, **(then) you**'ll grow up big and strong.'

- 'Spending time with experts **makes** you even better.'

- '**As you** ponder how to break into the new market segment, **you will** gain an even greater understanding of the market.'

As with mind reads, people can sometimes use causations in ways that are limiting. In such situations, we can probe the statements using questions which either to seek specific evidence or find counter-examples. Here are some examples:

- 'He **makes** me upset.'

Probe with: 'How specifically does he make you upset?', or 'how does what he's doing make you feel upset?' (specific evidence).

- '**If** you don't get to bed by 10pm, **then** you won't play well tomorrow.'

  Probe with: 'How do you know?', or 'according to whom?', or 'I went to bed after 10pm last week and played brilliantly the next day' (counter-example).

- '**If** you don't make 100 sales calls this week, **then** you won't meet your targets.'

  Probe with: 'How do you know?', or 'who says?' (specific evidence) or 'I met my targets last week and only made 50 calls.' (counter-example).

Notice that in the responses we are questioning whether something actually causes or leads to what the person thinks it does.

Equivalences

Equivalences are words/phrases that indicate that something *is* or *means* something, which may be true for the speaker and is almost certainly *not* the only possible interpretation of the events or situation.

We can create equivalences as follows: (the key equivalence words are shown in bold):

- 'Passing your exams **means** you'll be successful.'

- 'You **are** a lovely person.'

- 'Practising **is** the best way to learn.'

- 'Selling the most computers last year **means** we are the best.'

People can sometimes use equivalences in ways that are limiting. In such situations, we can probe the statements using questions which seek specific evidence or find counter-examples. Here are some examples:

- 'My boss yelling **means** she is annoyed with me.'

  Probe with: 'How does her yelling mean she is annoyed?' (specific evidence) or 'Have you ever yelled and not been annoyed?'(counter-example).

- 'My boss **is** nasty for shouting.'

  Probe with: 'How does shouting mean he is nasty? (specific evidence) or 'My boss shouts when his is passionate about a topic, and he is lovely' (counter-example).

- 'His being late **means** he doesn't care.'

  Probe with: 'How does his being late mean (specifically) that he doesn't care?' (specific evidence) or 'Have you ever been late for someone or something that you really cared about?' (counter-example).

Notice how in the responses we are questioning whether something actually does mean what the person thinks it means.

Anonymous judgements

Anonymous judgements are where we state that something 'is' good/bad/right/wrong, or some other value judgement, without explaining how we came to that conclusion. We create anonymous judgements using phrases such as:

- '**It is good** to be curious.'
- '**That's a wonderful thing** you just did.'
- '**It's perfect.**'
- '**That's the best way.**'
- '**It's important** to learn.'

These judgements can indicate beliefs that we have. Sometimes people use judgements in a way that is limiting. You can question the judgement by using phrases like, *'Who says...?'*, *"according to whom?'* and *'How do you know (specifically) that ...?'* (**Please remember** to use common sense and be in Rapport!) For example:

- **'It's bad** to be different.'

  Question the judgement with: 'How (specifically) do you know it's bad to be different?' or 'Who says it's bad?'

- **'It's good** to keep challenging your boss.'

  Question the judgement with: 'How do you know it's good to do that?'

- **'It's best** to not to complain when things are going wrong.'

  Question the judgement with: 'How do you know that?' or 'Who says it's best not to complain?'

Notice that in questioning the statements, we are essentially checking how the person making the judgement has come to that conclusion, which in turn may lead the person to reconsider the judgements they have made.

The language of generalisation

A generalisation is when we take one piece of data or information and assume that other things within that category are the same or that the pattern will be repeated. There are two main generalisation patterns to consider:

1. Universals

2. Rules

Universals

A universal is where we assume that an idea or concept applies (or does not apply) universally. These universals can have the effect of stopping us from searching for counter-examples, and hence they can limit our thinking.

We can create universals using words such as *all, everyone, everything, always, never, no one, nobody*, for example:

- 'We **all** want to succeed.'

- 'You **always** do your best.'

- 'You treat **everyone** with respect, and so **no one** disrespects you.'

- 'She **never** lets the team down.'

We sometimes hear people use universals in a limiting way. We can probe by asking for or providing counter-examples, or by asking the person to consider the consequences of the opposite. For example:

- 'We **never** buy from new suppliers.'

  Probe with: 'Never? Surely every new supplier was new at some time?' or 'What would happen if you did buy from a new supplier?'

- '**No one** talks to me at work.'

  Probe with: 'No one? You mean no one says a word to you all day, every day? Surely someone speaks to you?'

- 'She **always** wants to argue with me.'

  Probe with: 'Always? I heard you both laughing and joking together yesterday.'

- 'Have you noticed how **everyone** seems to be so disrespectful nowadays?'

  Probe with: 'Is everyone is like that? A few people perhaps, but most of the people I meet are just getting on with their life.'

Rules

We all (yes, *all* of us) have 'rules' in our mind about the way things are, should be or could be. These rules are indicated by words such as *should/shouldn't, ought/ought not, must/must not, has to/has not to, got to/got to not* and *need to/need to not*. These words indicate a sense of obligation or necessity. Other more relaxed forms of rules are more related to what is or is not possible, such as *can/can't, could/couldn't* and *might/might not*.

Examples of language indicating rules are:

- 'You **ought to** clinch the deal today.'

- 'We **must** remember how well we have done and how much we have learned.'

- 'You **can** pass all your exams.'

- 'This **might not** be as difficult as people think.'

- 'You **could** even get promoted.'

If these rules limit us, we can probe by asking questions that help people think of the consequences of the rule not actually being true, or even how to 'break' the (non-existent) rule. Here are some examples:

- 'I **can't** ask my boss for a pay rise.'

  Probe with: 'What stops you?' or 'What would happen if you did?'

- 'We **have** to invite our distant relatives to the wedding.'

  Probe with: 'Or...?' or 'What would happen if we didn't?'

- 'I **couldn't** ask her for a date.'

  Probe with: 'What stops you?' or 'What would happen if you did?'

The language of deletion

Every sentence has some information that is missing or deleted, and if we want to be incredibly detailed we could ask a huge number of questions about *who, what, where, when* and *how*, which could really annoy people. It is important when information is 'deleted' that we use our common sense and ask only questions that seek useful information.

There are four main deletion language patterns to consider:

1. Unspecified verbs, adverbs, adjectives

2. Abstract nouns

3. Unspecified comparisons

4. Unspecified people

Unspecified verbs, adverbs and adjectives

Almost any verb, adverb or adjective could be unspecified in certain contexts. Here are some examples:

- **'Continue** to **learn'** (It is not specified how we should continue, and what to learn).

- **'Be good'** (It is not specified how one should 'be good', and what constitutes 'good').

- 'You **look happy'** (It is not specified how exactly the person looks happy).

If it would be useful in a particular situation to 'probe', we could do so by asking questions to uncover relevant information. For example:

- 'Fred **ignored** me.'

  Probe with: 'How specifically did he ignore you?' or 'What exactly did he do/not do?'

- 'I am **uncomfortable**.'

  Probe with: 'About what?'

- 'Susan **rejected** me.'

  Probe with: 'How did she reject you?' or 'What did she do or not do, specifically?'

Abstract nouns

We'll often hear people use abstract nouns such as *communication, success, information, relationship, fulfilment, satisfaction* and *knowledge.* These nouns are intangible – we can't touch or see them. Because they are so abstract, they will mean different things to different people (we're back to 'a fair taxation system').

Examples of sentences with abstract nouns are:

- 'The **communication** here is excellent.'

- 'We all want **success**, don't we?'

- 'We are developing a great **relationship**.'

With many of these abstract words, they are processes/verbs which have been made into a noun, for example *communication* comes from the process of *communicating, relationship* comes from the process of *relating,* etc. If it would helpful to uncover more information, we can do so by turning the noun back into a process, for example:

- 'The **communication** here is really bad.'

  Turn back into a noun by saying: 'Who is not communicating to who?' or 'How would you like people to communicate instead?'

- 'The **relationship** needs improving.'

  Turn back into a noun by saying: 'How would you like us to relate differently?' or 'How can we change the way we relate?'

- I need more **knowledge** before I can answer that.'

  Turn back into a noun by saying: 'What (specifically) would you like/need to know?'

  Other ways are simply to ask for more specificity in the question, for example:

- 'We need more **information**.'

  Simply ask: 'What specific information would you like?'

Unspecified comparisons

These are when there is an explicit or implicit comparison being made, and there is no mention of what it is being compared to. These language patterns are often used effectively in advertising slogans, for example:

- 'Our brand washes **whiter**'

- 'We give you **more**'

- 'We deliver **faster**'

The slogans do not say what their product is being compared to.

When comparisons are made and it would be useful to understand against who/what/where/when the comparison is being made, you can ask the person to specify more information, for example:

- 'That's **expensive**.'

  Specify the information with: 'Compared to what?' (This can be an excellent way to handle objections when selling.)

- 'You're **slower**.'

  Specify the information with: 'Compared to who?' or 'Compared to when?'

- 'Our computers are **faster**.'

Specify the information with: 'Faster than whose?' or 'Faster than what?'

Unspecified People

Sometimes in sentences where people are mentioned it is not clear who is being talked about. If it would be useful to clarify, here are some examples of how to do so:

- 'They don't listen.'

  Clarify with: 'Who (specifically) doesn't listen?'

- 'People aren't respectful here.'

  Clarify with: 'Who specifically isn't respectful?'

- 'Can you do that, please.'

  Clarify with: 'Is the 'you' just one person' (or does the speaker mean more than one person, and if so, who?) or 'what exactly is the "that"?'

- 'We are going to do that?'

  Clarify with: 'Who exactly is "we"?'

Practical points about language patterns

You may find that some sentences have more than one deletion, distortion or generalisation. Which do you probe, and in what order? Firstly, as ever, use your common sense and consider the context and the purpose/outcome for asking the question.

As a general rule, distortions are more powerful filters than generalisations, which in turn are more powerful than deletions. My tip would be to probe distortions, and if there are no significant ones, probe generalisations and if there are no significant ones, probe deletions.

STORIES, ANALOGIES AND METAPHORS

The final topic in this chapter on language is about stories. Stories, analogies and metaphors are really useful ways to help people remember what you've told them (that's why this book has real life examples in each chapter) and also to overcome/displace resistance.

If someone says that they can't do something, if we simply tell them, 'oh yes you can/will/must,' it is unlikely to convince them that it is possible. However, if we tell a story or give an example about someone we know (or know of) who was in a broadly similar (or even worse) situation and how they managed to succeed, it will often displace resistance because it is about a third person, dissociated from the person you are speaking to.

Milton Erickson used metaphors extensively in his hypnotherapy practise. He also used abstract language to create a trance state. Grinder and Bandler modelled his language patterns and called it The Milton Model (see the *References and further reading* section for references on the use of metaphors, The Milton Model both generally and also specifically for selling).

 ACTION POINT

Take one of the language topics covered in this chapter and decide the best and most appropriate way for you to improve your use of that topic and then do it. For example, if you are taking the topic 'mind reads', listen out for the mind reads that people use on a given day, and either probe or question those mind reads using the relevant questions (where appropriate) or simply make a mental note of the question you would ask.

Repeat this exercise for each of the other language topics. If you take one topic per day, and revisit it, within a short time your capability will have increased significantly.

QUICK RECAP

- *Language is a very important topic, and the benefits of practising using the language patterns and tips shown in this chapter are immense.*
- *Language can be abstract or detailed, and the questions covered in the Hierarchy of Ideas help us to gain greater levels of abstraction (Chunking up), greater levels of details (Chunking down) or to think laterally.*
- *Remember, we all use the language patterns mentioned in this chapter anyway. The purpose of this chapter is to help you be even more aware of them than you have already been.*
- *We all use the language of Distortions, Deletions and Generalisations, and we can probe or question other people's language to uncover unspoken meaning.*
- *When questioning and using the Hierarchy of Ideas and The Meta Model, please remember to use common sense, make sure you are in Rapport, and resist any possible temptation to 'do NLP to someone'.*

PART 3

CHANGING BEHAVIOURS – THE NUTS AND BOLTS OF NLP

PART 3

CHAPTER 8

Being true to yourself: alignment

This chapter will explore a model that is widely used in NLP to identify and utilise the different levels of communication. It is known as Neurological Levels, sometimes abbreviated to Logical Levels. This model can help an individual or organisation to create a kind of 'alignment' which allows them to be totally focused and committed to their role. There are several ways to use this model. In this chapter we will cover the following four uses:

- Making changes and decisions
- Personal and organisational alignment
- Becoming even better at something, for example, being a leader
- Giving and receiving feedback

WHY IS THE LOGICAL LEVELS MODEL SO USEFUL?

The Logical Levels model was developed by Robert Dilts (one of the early students of NLP, who worked closely with Grinder and Bandler). Dilts based this model on work done by Gregory Bateson, a leading anthropologist who also greatly influenced Grinder and Bandler. This model can help individuals and organisations to create this 'alignment', and at the very least identify where there is an 'out of alignment'.

Have you noticed how some people, and indeed some organisations, seem to be 'aligned', in that they really are congruent (ie committed to and having their total energy focused on) in what they are doing. These individuals are often described as 'having charisma', 'knowing what they are about', and are rarely deflected from going for what they want. Signs of aligned organisations are that there are few internal politics, they focus on the customers and getting the job done efficiently, and everyone knows their role and what is expected of them. The Logical Levels model helps individuals and organisations to achieve this kind of alignment.

Some other benefits of this model are:

- The identification and resolution of 'problems' or challenges when managing or coaching.

- Assisting the planning and implementation of change management programmes at work.

- Helping to clarify and crystallise our thinking about situations.

- Providing us with a framework to improve as a leader, manager, coach or parent.

- Providing a framework for considering the ecology of any changes we wish to make.

- Providing a framework for giving and receiving feedback at work.

THE MODEL

Returning to the sentence, 'I can't do that here', let's consider six possible interpretations:

- If the emphasis is on *'here'*, it implies that there is something about the place or the *environment* ie 'I could do it elsewhere, but not here'. A relevant question would be 'where?'

- If the emphasis is on *'that'*, it implies that I don't know what *behaviours* to do. A relevant question would be 'what?', ie 'what to do?'

- If the emphasis is on *'do'*, it implies that I don't have the *skills/abilities/capabilities* to do it. I don't know *'how'* to do it.

- If the emphasis is on *'can't'*, it implies that I don't *believe* I can do it, and/or it is not important to me and doesn't fit with my values. In other words, I don't have reasons *'why'* to do it.

- If the emphasis is on *'I'*, it implies that I am not the sort of person to do this, that it doesn't fit with my *identity* or sense of self. *'Who'* am I to do this?

- A further possibility is that it doesn't fit with my sense of *purpose* or my *mission*. Purpose is about considering *'who else'* is affected.

This can be summarised in the diagram on the next page:

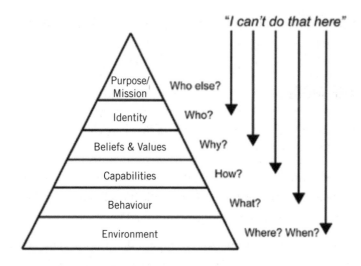

In a work context, *behaviours* and *capabilities* are often referred to as 'competencies'.

The following section explains the significance of each of these levels, and later in the chapter we will consider the relative importance of the levels and how to use the model.

How to recognise the various levels

People's language can highlight which level they are thinking at. Just as individuals operate at these various levels, so to do organisations (which is not surprising given that organisations are simply a collection of individuals). The table below gives some illustrations in the context of work and recreation:

Level	Examples of Relevant Statements
Purpose/Mission	• My company's mission is to provide solutions for all our clients • By keeping fit as I grow older, I become a role model for my children and grandchildren
Identity	• I am a good leader • I am a fit, healthy person

Beliefs & Values	• It's important that people feel valued at work • Fitness and recreation is important to me as it helps keep me healthy
Capability	• I am able to listen effectively to different points of view • I have a great serve in tennis
Behaviour	• I always make eye contact with the speaker in meetings • I bounce the ball three times before I serve
Environment	• I like the space in my new office • I like the scenery at my tennis club

How to use Logical Levels

There are several ways to use this model. We will cover the following four uses:

• Making changes and decisions

• Personal and organisational alignment

• Becoming even better at something, for example, being a leader

• Giving and receiving feedback

All of these uses are based on considering some or all of the levels in relation to each other, and in relation to the desired goals. To the extent that all the levels support, are supported by, and are in alignment with each of the other levels and our goals, we will feel and display a sense of congruency and alignment. We will be 'walking our talk' (ie our behaviours/actions will be in alignment with our words). For example, charismatic leaders will probably have a sense of purpose that is in alignment with who they feel they are (identity), and their beliefs, values and competencies as a leader will be complementary with each other and with the sense of identity and purpose, and the environment they operate in will reflect that.

Useful questions for each of the levels

The table below gives a selection of useful questions and tips for each level. These questions will be useful in the four uses we will cover. This is not an exhaustive list – feel free to adapt them to suit your own situation. Not all will be relevant to your situation.

Level	Examples of Useful Questions and Tips
Purpose/ Mission	• What is your mission in life/in this situation? • Who else are you 'serving', or responsible for? Who else is affected by your actions? • How do you want to be remembered when this situation is finished? What contribution will you have made? What legacy will you leave? • What is your sense of connection to the wider picture, perhaps some sort of 'spiritual' aspect?
Identity	• What is your sense of self in this situation (eg your sense of self as a leader?) • What sort of person (leader, parent) are you? • Could you describe yourself using an analogy, such as 'I am like a lion.' What analogy would you use for yourself?
Beliefs & Values	• What's important to you? • Do these values clash with things which are important to you in other areas of your life (eg work-life balance)? • What do you believe about this situation? • What empowering beliefs do you have about yourself and/or your capabilities in this situation? • What disempowering beliefs do you have about yourself in this situation? Are these disempowering beliefs actually 100% true? If you gained additional skills, would these disempowering beliefs change? If so, how could you gain these skills? Who could help you? • What do you believe about other people involved?

Capability	• What skills and abilities do you have that are relevant/useful in this context? • What skills would be useful to learn or adopt? Do you have these skills in other contexts, and how could you transfer them? • How could you learn new relevant skills? • How do you communicate? What communication skills do you have, and which ones would be worth developing? • What capabilities does this organisation want to develop and encourage? How would these be demonstrated in behaviours?
Behaviour	• What are/will you be doing? • Consider what actions you are or will be taking. • What behaviours do you use in other situations that may be useful here? • What behaviours are not useful in this context? • What behaviours do you want to encourage/discourage? (Particularly useful for teams, organisations and HR departments.)
Environment	• Where do you work? • Where does/will XX take place? • Describe the current surroundings. How would you like them to be? • Who is/will be around you/with you? • How long does it take to reach the 'place' (eg office, hotel)?

Making changes and decisions

As a generalisation, the higher the Logical Level, the more impact change at that level will have on the person or organisation, and it will tend to affect levels lower down. For example, if we change our values and beliefs, so that something becomes important, even if we don't have the skills and abilities to do it, because it is important we will go and learn how to do it.

🔍 EXAMPLE

I ran a brief workshop where a lady wanted to be able to make cold calls (ie behaviour *and/or* capability *levels). She had been having difficulty starting the process. On probing, it became clear that she had some 'limiting' beliefs about cold-calling. During the workshop I helped her to change her beliefs about cold calling, so that she believed it was a useful thing to do as opposed to her previous belief that it was a bad thing to do (changing* beliefs *and* values*). After that, she congruently said that even though she wasn't sure about the best way to make cold calls (ie* behaviours *and* capabilities*), she would go and find out. So changing her* beliefs *and* values *impacted on lower levels.*

As a further generalisation, if we can identify the Logical Level at which the 'problem' is held, change will be easier if we can address it either at that level or at higher levels. If a staff member says, 'I can't do presentations here', sending them on a Powerpoint or presentation course (which normally address *behaviours* and/ or *capabilities*) will be a complete waste of time and money if the person does not believe that presentations are important (*beliefs/values*), or feel that they are not the sort of person to make presentations (*identity*). Managers and HR professionals please take note of this.

It is hard to imagine a successful work-based change management project being successful unless each of the six levels were considered and addressed.

When making important decisions, spending a little time considering the situation from each of the different levels (perhaps by using some of the questions in the table on p.124) will normally pay dividends.

PERSONAL (AND ORGANISATIONAL) ALIGNMENT

We can use the questions and principles of Logical Levels, and the information in the table on p.124, to assist us as individuals (and also organisations and teams) to become more aligned. In short, we can use the questions to help ensure that all of the levels support each other. To the extent that there is alignment and focus, individuals and organisations will be more likely to achieve goals than if there is lack of alignment, and often organisations will need fewer people to achieve their goals because everyone is pulling in the same direction. For example:

- Is our sense of purpose in line with our sense of self/identity?

- Is our sense of self in alignment with what is important to us and what we believe?

- Are our beliefs and values in line with our skills and the behaviours we adopt?

- Are our skills supported by appropriate behaviours, and do our behaviours reflect our skills?

- Is the environment we operate in a good reflection of us, who we are, our skills and values, and where we want to be?

- Do we 'walk our talk'?

- Is all of this in line with our goals?

TOP TIPS

Greater alignment increases the chance that individuals and organisations will achieve goals and that it will be a 'pleasant' journey.

BECOMING EVEN BETTER

We can use this model if we want to be even better at something, for example, being a leader, manager or coach. This is best explained by way of an exercise.

✍ ACTION POINT

This exercise has several steps, and is summarised diagrammatically at the end. It typically takes 15–20 minutes to do. It may be helpful to ask a trusted friend or colleague to assist you. Their role is to ask the questions and write the answers, **not** to engage in conversation, coach you or give their opinion.

1. Choose the area or skill you would like to become even better at. On the floor mark out five spaces in a line with five pieces of paper – one each for *environment (E), behaviour (B), capability (C), beliefs and values (B&V)* and *identity (I)*. Leave a space after *identity* for *purpose/mission*. Have the pieces approximately one pace apart.

2. Starting at *environment*, ask yourself some of the relevant environment questions from the table on p.125. For example, 'where am I a leader?' Allow yourself enough time to answer the question properly.

3. When you have answered that, step forward into the *behaviour* space. Ask yourself the relevant behaviour questions from the table, for example, 'what (behaviours) do I do as a leader?' Allow yourself sufficient time to answer.

4. Continue for *capability* (eg 'how do I lead?' or 'what skills and abilities do I have as a leader?'), *beliefs and values* (eg 'why do I lead', 'what's important to me as a leader?', 'what do I believe as a leader?'), and *identity* (eg 'who am I as a leader?', 'what's my sense of self as a leader?').

5. Step forward beyond *identity* into *purpose/mission*. Continue to face away from the five previous spaces, and ask yourself questions such as, 'what's my mission/purpose as a leader? Who else am I serving as a leader?' Again, allow yourself time to process your thoughts.

6. Turn round so that you are facing the five spaces, and reflect on how your mission impacts on the five levels.

7. When you are ready take this sense of purpose/mission/ connectedness and step forward into the *identity* space. Ask yourself, 'who am I now as a leader? What's my sense of self now, as a leader?'

8. When you have finished, step forward into *beliefs and values*. 'What's important to me now, what do I now believe, as a leader?'

9. When you have finished, step forward into *capability*. 'What skills do I now have, or which ones would I want to acquire, as a leader?'

10. When you have finished, step forward into *behaviour*. 'What behaviours do I now have, or which ones would I want to acquire/change, as a leader?'

11. Step forward into *environment*. 'Where do I lead?', 'where else do I lead?', 'where else could I lead?', 'what changes could I make in my environment?'

12. Finally, step a few paces off to the side and look at the Logical Levels ladder again. Ask yourself 'What have I taken from this exercise? What will I do differently as a leader? How will I be different as a leader?'

Diagrammatically, the pieces of paper should look like this:

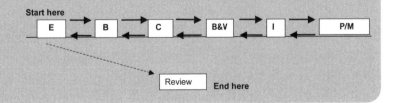

GIVING AND RECEIVING FEEDBACK

Giving and receiving feedback can sometimes be challenging if it highlights areas for improvement. One of the main reasons for this is that some people (both givers and receivers of feedback) don't know how to do it effectively. One of the main reasons for this is that they confuse *behaviours*, which is what feedback should cover, with either *capabilities* or *identity*, or both.

Givers of feedback (often managers) sometimes make negative comments about a staff member's capabilities (eg 'you didn't present very well') or identity (eg 'you are not a good presenter') rather than behaviours (eg the level of eye contact, or distracting movements when presenting).

Similarly, some staff members distort comments about behaviours that their boss would like them to change (eg 'keep your hands still the next time you present, and make sure you look people in the eye') as meaning that they personally (ie at identity level) need to change or are in some way not good enough (eg 'I can't present well', or even 'I am not a good presenter').

TOP TIPS

As managers, when mentioning areas for improvement as part of feedback to individuals, it is usually best to make it clear that it is at behavioural level, and to use language (see the tables on p.122 and p.124 for guidelines) that reflects this.

QUICK RECAP

- *The Logical Levels model has six levels – purpose/mission, identity, beliefs and values, capabilities, behaviours and environment.*
- *It is an extremely useful model to help us structure our thinking, and gain increased personal or organisational alignment.*
- *The model can be used as a guide to problem-solving, by looking at which level(s) the problem arises and then dealing with it at either that level or a higher one. Similarly, possible solutions can be evaluated by using this model.*
- *It can also be used as a way to make changes or decisions.*
- *The model can be used to become even better as a manager, leader or coach.*
- *Generally, ask for changes to be made at* behavioural *level when giving feedback to individuals.*

CHAPTER 9

How to be in *the* right state: managing your emotions

Many people get nervous or experience some form of negative emotion or state in certain situations or at certain times. Sometimes people may feel good in certain situations, and would like to feel even better so that they can perform to their best, for example in a sporting competition or an interview. In Chapter 2 we discussed the Communication Model and the importance of state. In this chapter, we will cover how to manage your state so that you can be in *the* right state rather than *a* right state.

CONTROLLING YOUR STATE

In NLP there is probably only one equation to be aware of:

Present State + Resources = Desired State

If we are feeling anxious about a situation and we add resources such as feeling motivated, powerful, confident, relaxed, happy, anticipation, energised and focused (normally two or three will be sufficient), we will be in the state that we want to be in. This list of states is by no means exhaustive – we can choose whichever states we want, as we will cover a little later in this chapter.

We gain access to resources such as these by a process called anchoring. This also links back to one of the NLP presuppositions: 'we all have the untapped potential to achieve more.'

An Anchor is a term used in NLP to describe a stimulus that leads to a response. Probably the most well-known early exponent of the principles of what we now call anchoring is Russian doctor Ivan Pavlov and his experiments with dogs in the early 20th century, where he repeatedly rang a bell, showed his dogs some meat and they salivated. After a while, the dogs salivated at the sound of the bell without the presence of the meat.

Anchors occur naturally in many different aspects of our lives, and occur in any of our five senses. Hearing the first few bars from our favourite up-beat dance song will probably make us feel energised. The first few bars from a mellow song, however, will probably have a calming effect. Seeing the face of a friend or close relative will make us feel happy. Seeing the face of someone we don't like will have the opposite effect. The same principles apply for kinaesthetic (for example holding a small baby), olfactory (for example smelling certain aftershaves or perfumes) and gustatory (for example tasting certain foods). Advertisers use the principal of stimulus-response with their advertising jingles and catch-phrases.

In essence the theory of anchoring is simple. If we can link the state that we want to access to a particular stimulus (a picture, sound, physical movement, taste or smell, or some combination of these), then when we replicate this stimulus we will *immediately* get into the desired state.

Why learn to control your state?

A more sensible question would be, 'why *not* learn to manage your state?' There are numerous situations where being able to control your state is useful, for example before or during interviews, sports competitions, presentations, difficult meetings, appraisals, exams and even when asking your boss for a pay rise. Managing our state helps us to be more in charge of our responses and hence our results.

ACTION POINT

Make a list of situations that might cause you some unease (such as interviews, presentations and sports matches), and list the resources/states that you would like to have access to ie how you would prefer to feel.

How do we use anchors?

It is possible to set anchors for other people, or to help them to set anchors for themselves. In this book we will concentrate on setting anchors for us personally. We will cover how to set a 'stacked resource anchor', in other words repeating the anchoring process several times so that the anchor is both very strong and contains one or more desired resources/states. The process is relatively straightforward, and normally takes between 10 and 15 minutes.

As a note of caution, anchors are excellent for relatively mild negative experiences that are in specific contexts. They are **not** for dealing with very strong negative emotions such as phobias, anger, persistent anxiety or grief. If we wish to deal with these latter situations it is important to find NLP or other professionals specifically qualified to deal with these sorts of strong emotions.

SETTING A RESOURCE ANCHOR

Given that anchors can occur in any one or more of the five senses, when we are setting an anchor for ourselves we can choose which one(s) are most suitable for us and the situation(s) we will find ourselves in. This will become clearer later in this chapter. There are five keys to successful anchoring, and seven steps to setting the anchor. Let's consider the five keys first.

The five keys to anchoring

Here are some of the key points to take into account when doing the anchoring process.

1. **Intensity**: if we create an anchor from really powerful intense experiences when we felt, for example, extremely motivated, we will be able to replicate this level of motivation. If we use an example of when we felt just a little motivated, that's all we will be able to re-create when we 'fire' (ie activate or trigger) the anchor.

2. **Timing**: when setting the anchor we need to capture the peak of the experience. The diagram on p.137 shows that when we relive a given event the intensity of the emotion/ state will rise and then fall back to our natural, 'baseline' state. If we capture the peak of the state (between the two dotted vertical lines) by setting or applying the anchor as the state nears its peak and then releasing the anchor just after

the peak (by following the seven steps to anchoring) we can create a very powerful anchor for ourselves. Typically the period where someone is 'in state' when setting the anchor lasts between 5 and 15 seconds. This is a guideline – we are all unique individuals – for some people this peak lasts a second or two, for others up to a minute or even longer.

The anchoring process

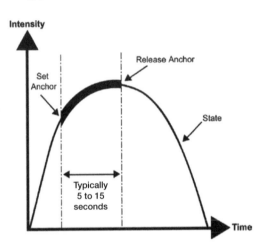

3. **Uniqueness** of the anchor: the stimulus should be unique so that it is easy to set and will not be fired/activated accidentally. Anchors on the palm of the hand, for example, will be constantly triggered when shaking hands and will probably lose their impact, whereas squeezing the tip of your thumb and index finger on your right hand or squeezing your wedding ring are probably unique movements for most people.

4. **Replicability** of the anchor: This ensures that you can fire the anchor whenever you need to. Holding your left big toe is probably unique but not replicable before or during

an interview. Pressing your thumb and index finger together is probably replicable during most situations – other people present would probably not notice you doing it, and even if they did would not think twice about it.

5. **Number of times** the anchoring is done: when doing the anchoring process, typically doing it between three and six times will be more powerful and effective than doing it once or twice.

A useful mnemonic to remember is **ITURN (Intensity, Timing, Uniqueness, Replicability, Number).**

TOP TIPS

It is important to stress that anchoring is about *states* and *emotions*. Check that it really is a state that has some intensity. For example, feeling 'efficient' is probably not an intense experience. How do you feel when you feel efficient? If the reply is, 'strong and powerful', accompanied by an intense feeling and physiological shift, this suggests that 'strong and powerful' are appropriate states to be anchored.
If the states that you want seem 'contradictory' or mutually exclusive, for example being 'calm' and being 'energised', then ask yourself whether you can be in both states at the same time. If you believe you can, then do the process as outlined above. If not, then create two sets of anchors – one an 'up-time' anchor and the other a 'chill-out' anchor. Do both in the same way, but separately and using different physical anchors for the 'up-time' and 'chill-out' anchors (for example different hands, or different fingers on the same hand).

If it is more appropriate to set an auditory anchor, you could perhaps remember a piece of music in your mind, or even say a phrase to yourself, such as, 'go for it'. Do not rely on an externally generated sound, like your coach's voice – he or she may not be there every time you need it. Similarly with a visual anchor, make it something that you can see in your mind rather than see externally. You can use a combination of two or more senses. However, for many people, the physical movement is normally sufficient and extremely effective, especially since auditory and visual anchors can be disturbed by the sights and sounds of the events happening when you want to fire the anchor.

The seven steps to anchoring

There are seven steps to setting an anchor:

1. **Ensure you are clear** on the process that you will take yourself through (ie these seven steps), and decide on the desired states to be anchored and how you will anchor it (physical movement, sound, picture or a combination). Ensure also that you do an ecology check regarding the consequences of doing this process, and that you know what you want from the process (ie the first point from the Principles for Success).

2. **Recall** a vivid past experience of an event where you felt one of the desired states from step one eg confident, motivated, powerful. Pick one state at a time, eg confident, and then one past experience at a time that relates to that state.

3. Make sure you are really **associated** into that event, in other words you are reliving it as if you were there right now, not merely thinking about it. See what you are seeing (ie as if it were happening right now because you are fully associated into the event), hear what you are hearing and really feel the feelings of being totally confident (for example).

4. **Anchor**; ie apply the stimulus (for example pressing your thumb and index finger together), at the peak of the experience (see the diagram on p.137).

5. **Change state**, ie think about something neutral.

6. **Repeat** steps 2 to 5 three to six times as necessary. Use the same anchor (eg thumb and index finger each time – this is known as Stacking anchors).

7. **Test** by firing/activating the anchor, eg pressing your thumb and index finger together.

If you cannot think of a time when you felt, for example, confident, give yourself a little time. Sometimes people cannot immediately come up with a situation, but when they think of one, other memories start flooding back. If that does not work, pretend! Our unconscious mind does not know the difference between an actual event and a vividly imagined one.

TOP TIPS Even though an anchor that is created well can last a long time (sometimes permanently), it is often useful to 'top-up' the anchor regularly, and certainly whenever a really good positive experience happens to you.

Test (step 7) after about three (of the six) sets of anchoring. This lets you know whether you are on track. If by some chance there is little or no change when you fire the anchor, re-read the process and pay particular attention to make sure that:

• You are actually reliving the experience rather than thinking about it.

• You are reliving one experience at a time, not two or three experiences.

- You really want to do this process – is there any reason why you would not want to? What are the reasons for doing process, and how will it benefit you?

Future Pacing

If you have set an anchor for a specific event, such as an interview, an additional element to incorporate in step 7 is something known as Future Pacing. This is when we envisage ourselves in the situation having done the anchoring (or whichever NLP technique we have been doing), and notice how things are different in our minds now. This is akin to mental rehearsal done by successful sports people.

When we future pace the resource anchor, it is useful to do two types of mental rehearsal. The first is Dissociated, in other words seeing ourselves at the interview as if on a TV or cinema screen. We fire our anchor, and at the same time see ourselves in the picture with the resources anchored. The second type is Associated, in other words imagining we are in the situation as if looking through our own eyes, again with the anchor fired. In both forms, we can do it with our eyes open or closed.

With dissociated mental rehearsal, we can often notice aspects of how we are behaving, what we are doing or not doing to help the situation go well. Some people find one type more useful than the other. Find which type(s) work best for you.

An additional point when future pacing is that it is helpful is to consider several different scenarios, and in each scenario we are feeling the anchored state and hence 'performing' the way we want. The benefit of future pacing different scenarios is that we can be prepared for all eventualities, not just preparing for things going perfectly (interviewers and audiences sometimes ask challenging questions, sporting conditions and opponents are not always how we would wish them to be). So we would do dissociated future pacing on several scenarios with our anchor fired, and then a few seconds after we have finished repeat it for associated future pacing.

Q EXAMPLE

In their book Mind Games – Inspirational Lessons From The World's Biggest Sports Stars, *Jeff Grout and Sarah Perrin mention that Sally Gunnell, winner of a gold medal at 1992 Barcelona Olympic Games, mentally rehearsed success under numerous different scenarios. If things were going wrong in her mind's video, she would re-wind the film and replay it, winning every time.*

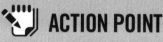 **ACTION POINT**

Revisit the exercise on p.139, and set a personal resource anchor. When setting the anchor, it will probably be easier if you find a quiet place where you know you will not be disturbed.

OTHER PRACTICAL USES OF ANCHORING

Apart from setting a personal resource anchor as described above you can create anchors for yourself in other ways. For example:

- Wearing your favourite item of clothing for an important interview

- Carrying a picture of a loved one and looking at it before the meeting

- Playing your favourite song on your personal stereo system (make sure the battery is charged!)

You can also create anchors in other people. Advertisers do it all the time. Many comedians, when they tell a punch line, will make a physical gesture and/or change their tone of their voice. These are anchors.

> **TOP TIPS**
>
> Music can be used as anchors. For example, you can use certain songs (for example, *I Feel Good* by James Brown) to create moods/states in audiences. When running meetings or training courses, you can use a certain song of your choice as the 'return to your seats' song. Certain phrases, such as, 'listen up' can be used to create a response.

Dealing with negative anchors

Just as anchors can be positive, so can other anchors be negative. There are techniques within NLP to help overcome these, and they are outside the scope of this book. You can read about how to deal with negative anchors (in NLP we call this Collapsing anchors) in some of the textbooks referred to in the *References and further reading* section.

QUICK RECAP

- *Setting Anchors is a simple and very effective way to manage your emotional State in many potentially challenging situations such as interviews, presentations, meetings and important sports competitions.*
- *Remember the ITURN (Intensity, Timing, Uniqueness, Replicability, Number) mnemonic when setting anchors.*
- *Following the seven steps to anchoring process outlined will help you create long-lasting Anchors.*
- *Mentally rehearsing an event beforehand will improve your chances of success. Do Dissociated and/or Associated mental rehearsal (whichever is useful for you), using several likely scenarios, with each scenario turning out the way you want it to.*
- *Remember to top up the Anchor, especially when something great happens to you.*

CHAPTER 10

How to really use your brain: changing your responses to situations

Have you ever wondered how you know that you like one food and yet dislike another? Or how you know that you look forward to doing one activity and dread another? Or that you believe something and no longer believe something else? What happens inside your head to let you know about these distinctions? Can we change our responses to events and situations, and if so, how? In this chapter we will address these questions.

MODALITIES AND SUBMODALITIES

You will remember from the Communication Model covered in Chapter 2 (p.19), and representational systems covered in Chapter 6 (p.81), that we have an internal representation of thoughts and external events, held in one or more of the five senses. Another word in NLP for representational system is Modality (visual modality, auditory modality etc).

For each of the modalities there are finer distinctions. For example, if we take visual, the internal picture we have of something could be big or small, bright or dim, near or far and a whole series of other distinctions. The same applies with the other senses, primarily auditory and kinaesthetic. In NLP, these finer distinctions of the modalities are called Submodalities. What Grinder and Bandler found was that these finer distinctions determine the meaning we place on things, and changing the submodalities of a given 'thing' changes its meaning. The submodalities could be called 'the brain's software', and by knowing how to use our own submodalities, we can help 'manage' our brain and our responses.

Why is this so useful?

We can use submodalities for a variety of purposes, for example:

- To make certain foods or drinks less appealing.

- To make certain activities more appealing, such as exercise, doing necessary paperwork (such as tax returns!), making cold calls.

- To help us feel more comfortable about certain 'pressure' situations, such as sporting competitions, presentations.

- To calm ourselves down if we are too 'psyched up'.

I have used this successfully when working with businesspeople and sports people. Students learning how to use this on my NLP courses have helped each other make significant changes.

Q EXAMPLE

On one NLP Practitioner course, a student helped a fellow student to feel comfortable about making cold calls, which he previously didn't like doing. (The approach they used is similar to that used in the example with Sally and Kelly on p.158 below.) After this 10 minute piece of work, he called himself 'the cold-calling monster', and won huge amounts of business from blue-chip companies from initial cold-calls.

Richard Bandler has likened our journey through life to being on a bus. The question he poses is, 'who is driving the bus?' Is it other people, or are we driving our own bus? The use of submodalities is one of the techniques that helps us to drive our own bus.

Please note that, as with anchoring, submodalities are to be used for relatively minor unwanted responses, **not** for major issues such as phobias, panics, depression, anger etc. As we covered in Chapter 9 (p.133), these issues are best referred to a suitably qualified professional.

A word about ecology

As you will remember from earlier chapters, whenever we want to make any changes using NLP it is essential to make sure that there are positive consequences and no significant negative consequences of doing so (on other aspects of your life, or on that of others) before making the change. Assuming they are heavily outweighed by positive consequences, very minor and short-term negative consequences may be acceptable. Please use your common sense when evaluating the consequences.

HOW DO WE USE SUBMODALITIES?

In this section, we will cover some basic points, before we move on to consider the process of how to use and change submodalities, so that we can change our experience of something, or our response to it.

Basic points

When you think of a particular thing, for example a food that you like, you will almost certainly have a picture of it in your mind, and there are maybe some sounds associated with the food, and also possibly some feelings. These pictures, sounds and feelings often happen so quickly and automatically that we are not normally consciously aware of it.

Working with submodalities is essentially a two part process. Firstly, identify or elicit the submodalities of a particular event or experience. Secondly, adjust the key submodalities to create the desired response. This will be covered further in the section headed *Working with submodalities.*

In order to use submodalities, we first need to start with having a list of what they are. Although we could get finer distinctions of olfactory/smell and gustatory/taste, generally we use only visual, auditory and kinaesthetic submodalities.

Here is a list of different submodalities:

Visual (regarding the picture)

Likely key submodalities
- Near or far
- Bright or dim
- Location in your visual field (eg high left, directly in front of you)
- Size of picture (big or small)
- Looking through your own eyes or seeing yourself in the picture (you will remember this from Chapter 9 (p.133) on anchoring as associated or Dissociated respectively)
- Focused or unfocused
- Moving or still
- If moving (fast/normal/slow)

Others
- Focus (changing or steady)
- Framed or panoramic/no frame
- Colour or black and white
- Amount of contrast (lots or none)
- 3D or flat
- Angle viewed from (eg straight ahead, looking down, looking up)
- Anything else that is particularly noticeable

Auditory (regarding the sound)

Likely key submodalities
- Location of sounds
- Direction if there is movement (eg towards you, clockwise by your right ear)
- Volume (loud or soft)
- Fast or slow

Others
- Pitch (high or low)
- Timbre (clear or raspy)
- Pauses
- Particular cadence or rhythm
- Notable duration of the sounds (eg long time, short time?)
- Uniqueness of sound
- Anything else that is particularly noticeable

> **Kinaesthetic (regarding the feeling)**
>
> *Likely key submodalities*
> - Location of the feeling (eg chest, stomach, neck)
> - Size (big or small)
> - Shape (eg round, oval, square, egg shaped)
> - Intensity (high or low)
> - Temperature (hot or cold)
> - Pressure (high or low)
> - Texture (rough or smooth)
> - Heavy or light
> - Still or moving
> - Movement (fast or slow)
>
> *Others*
> - Colour (even though this is a visual, some people say that the feeling/shape has a colour)
> - Intensity (steady or unsteady)
> - Duration (short or long)
> - Humidity (dry or wet)
> - Vibration
> - Inside or outside you
> - Anything else that is particularly noticeable

The above list is not exhaustive. It is perfectly possibly that there are other submodalities that are relevant for you. It is also perfectly possible that you may not have any sounds that are associated with, for example, the food, or even any feelings. Normally people will have a picture. Please note that because the visual representational system processes extremely quickly, you may not be immediately aware of the picture when you think of the food – sometimes you might want to take a moment to take a snapshot or catch the picture in your mind.

TOP TIPS

Generally, the visual submodalities will be the most important of all three modalities, although auditory and kinaesthetic can also be very important for some people.

When you listen to people speaking, often they will give clues to their submodalitites, (remember, language is a verbal expression of our internal representations). Here are some phrases that you will probably have heard people say (the submodalities will be shown in brackets for your reference):

- The dim and distant past *(visual: brightness, distance)*

- I have a big problem hanging over me *(visual: size, location)*

- That gives me a warm feeling inside (people often move their hands to indicate where the feeling is. *(kinaesthetic: temperature, location)*

- I hear it loud and clear *(auditory: volume)*

- I feel the pressure *(kinaesthetic: pressure)*

ACTION POINT

Choose one pleasant place or activity. Think of that place or activity and see the picture of it in your mind. Notice some of the main aspects of that picture – how big is the picture, where is it in relation to your visual field, the brightness of the picture, and some of the other submodalities that you notice. Ask yourself if there are any sounds that are important, and notice the main submodalities of the sound. Then check to see if there are feelings that are important, and notice the main submodalities. It may be useful to have someone with you who can ask you to tell them the key submodalities so that you are not distracted by having to make a note or remember them. Because our unconscious mind works quickly and we get internal representations very quickly, it's best to elicit submodalities very quickly. This exercise should take only around one or two minutes.

TOP TIPS

When noting the submodalities, the *content* of the picture (or sounds or feelings) is **not** important. It is the submodalities that are important. For example, when thinking of chocolate, having a picture in your mind of a bar of chocolate on a table is the content; the size of the picture or whether it is near or far are examples of submodalities. Remember, submodalities give meaning to our experience, they let us know whether we like or dislike something, believe or don't believe something etc. and it is the submodalities themselves, **not** the content, that does this.

Working with submodalities

Working with submodalities is a relatively simple process, with three main steps:

1. **Elicit** the (main) submodalities

2. **Find** the one(s) that are really important to you

3. **Change** them so that you feel the way you want to about that experience (eg, food, person, activity)

Eliciting

In the exercise on p.151, you elicited your own submodalities for a pleasant place or activity. The principles are the exactly same for eliciting the submodalities of something you want to change (for example, a food you like and wished you didn't or a feeling of nerves at the thought of a particular activity or person).

Finding the key submodalities

For most people, there will be one submodality which is so important that when the person changes that one, it impacts on all the others. In NLP we call these Drivers. The key submodalities in the tables earlier in this chapter are likely candidates to be drivers.

One way to find the driver is simply to change each of the submodalities in turn, starting with the visuals, and noticing which has the biggest impact. Drivers are most likely to be those submodalities where there is a spectrum, rather than an 'either/ or'. For example, a picture can be:

• Huge, tiny, or anything in between

• Very bright, very dim or anything in between

• Numerous different locations

• Very near, very far, or anything in between

But it can only be:

• Black and white or colour

• Framed or panoramic

• 3D or flat

And therefore these three latter submodalities are unlikely to be drivers, although they could be important for some people in certain contexts.

One possible exception is associated/dissociated. As you will see from the next chapter, and you may already have noticed this from your anchoring exercises, stepping into/out of the picture or the situation can have a significant impact on our experience.

✎ ACTION POINT

The purpose of this exercise is for you to understand which submodalities have the biggest impact for you in different contexts, so that you can adjust them if and when necessary to alter your experience or response.

1. Think of an activity or place you like.
2. Note the key 'spectrum' submodalities, especially the visual ones, plus any auditory or kinaesthetic which are particularly important.
3. Take one spectrum submodality at a time. For each one, change the submodality in one direction (for example, making the picture bigger than it was), and notice whether it makes the situation even better, or worse or has no impact. Then, move it in the opposite direction (in this case, making it smaller than it was) and notice the impact. Return it to its original size. Do the same for the others, eg location (choose different locations eg near to your right, far away to your left), brightness (even brighter, even dimmer), distance (closer, further away) etc, each time returning to the original location, brightness, distance etc.
4. Do the same as step 3 with the 'either/or' submodalities. It will only be possible to change them in one direction.
5. Notice which one has the biggest impact on your experience. Occasionally there may be more than one which has a big impact, and there will normally be one which has the biggest impact.
6. You may want to check this by taking a different example from the same context (eg activity) and change just the one or two submodalities in the direction that makes it *more pleasant* (from 4 above) and notice the impact. Do these one or two submodalities have a similar impact as in the first example? If not, repeat steps 3 and 4 to find which one or two have the biggest impact. Gain further insight by taking examples from a

different context (eg food, person) and noticing the impact of changing the key submodalities from previous examples. You may find that you have the same driver regardless of the topic or you may find that the driver is different for different topics.

Changing your experience

Once you have found your key submodalities, making changes to your experience becomes relatively easy. Simply pick a relatively minor unwanted response, such as:

- A food you like and wish you didn't like quite so much (or not at all). Remember ecology here. For example, if you are a vegetarian, and your main intake of protein is from cheese, and you want to eat far less cheese, where will you get your protein intake from?

- An activity that would benefit you if it were more appealing or if you felt more comfortable doing it (eg exercise, doing certain types of paperwork, making cold calls, doing presentations, interviews).

- A person who makes you feel a little uncomfortable in a specific context (eg partnering the club coach in a tennis doubles final).

Then, think of that situation, and change the driver(s), and notice the impact. Change the driver in such a way that it has the desired impact on the situation. For example, if your driver is 'distance', and you would like to feel more motivated to do paperwork, get a picture in your mind of doing paperwork and slightly alter the distance (bring it a little closer and then move it a little further away), and notice which creates the desired response. Remember the first Principle for Success – know what you want from the exercise before you start.

TOP TIPS

Generally, you will increase the impact of something by:

- Making a picture bigger, brighter, nearer, higher in your visual field, seeing it through your own eyes, moving faster and more focused.
- Making the sounds louder, faster, moving towards you.
- Making the feelings bigger, move faster, in a specific part of your body (it will vary from person to person, but often the chest or stomach).

And you will decrease the impact by:

- Making a picture smaller, dimmer, further away, lower in your visual field, seeing yourself in the picture rather than through your own eyes, putting a frame around it, making it black and white, moving slower and less focused.
- Making the sounds quieter, slower, moving away from you.
- Making the feelings smaller, move slower or stay still, in non-central parts of your body (it will vary from person to person, but often the elbow, knee, foot, or a different location to the place of intense feeling such as the chest/stomach).

If you have not found the driver(s), then you can still make desired changes to your response or the way you feel about something. You do this simply by 'trial and success', based on the process in the exercise on p.154. The following examples illustrate this point.

🔍 EXAMPLE

Nicki, a 19-year old tennis player reached the final of a mixed doubles tournament, and her partner was Robin, the club coach. The final was against a very good pair, and Nicki felt a little intimidated playing with Robin in important matches because he was the coach (note how this is a relatively minor 'problem' in a specific context – generally she got on very well with Robin). Nicki and I had only a few minutes together, and she knew the kind of work I did and asked for a bit of assistance in the few minutes we had. (I checked with Nicki that there would not be any negative consequences of doing this).

I did not have time to find the driver(s). I said to her, 'when you think of Robin, do you have a picture?' She said, 'Yes'. Knowing the likely key submodalities, I took each submodality in turn and asked her to change it and whether that made her feel better, worse or no change (I used the tips covered earlier as a guide, so making the picture smaller, dimmer etc, and to keep the changes that made her feel better). Although this improved the situation, she was still not feeling as she would have liked. We moved onto the auditory submodalities, and I repeated the process. For her, moving the sound a little further away and turning down the volume slightly (not too far, nor too low, as she said she wouldn't have been able to hear him at all and would have felt too distant), plus making the picture of him still and in a frame made her feel comfortable. I asked Nicki to lock in the changes (ie to keep the picture and sounds the way she had just changed them to be).

She told me the match went really well, and that she played really well and felt comfortable with Robin, and that, most importantly, they won!

With Nicki, had we had a little more time, I could probably have found the driver(s). The process we did took only about five minutes, and had she known what you now know, she could have done it herself.

With the next example, you will see that if you have a comparable desired situation, you can change the submodalities of the undesired situation to be those of the desired situation, thus giving it the same meaning as the desired situation. As you remember from earlier, submodalities determine the meaning we place on experiences. Changing submodalities changes the meaning of an event.

Q EXAMPLE

Sally, a coaching client, was a manager in a major FTSE 100 company. She said that there was one particular member of the management team, Kelly, who made her feel uncomfortable. I asked Sally to think of Kelly and to get a picture, and to notice the key things about the picture particularly location, size, brightness and focus, and then to think of someone on the team who she felt comfortable with and to do the same, and to notice which submodalities were different. For Sally, when she thought of Kelly the picture was bigger, higher and nearer than the second picture. I simply asked Sally to make the picture of the Kelly to be the same size and location (ie make it smaller, lower and further away) as that of the person she felt comfortable with. Having done that, and having lokced the changes in place, Sally said she felt the same way about Kelly as she did about the other members of the team. Sally mentioned that in the subsequent meetings with Kelly, she felt comfortable and didn't interpret Kelly's behaviour as being a problem at all.

The method outlined in the example above shows that if we have a desired situation that we would like to change the current situation to, it provides a set of submodalities that we can use as a 'target', so that we know, for example, how big or small to make the picture, exactly where to move it to, etc. This is the method used by one of my students to help a fellow student become a 'cold-calling monster' as outlined on p.147.

TOP TIPS

Whenever we use the method outlined in the example about Sally, it is essential that we use as a 'target' something of the same type, ie two foods, two people on the management team, two activities etc.

Any of the methods outlined in the exercises and examples can be used to change our experience of a relatively minor, unwanted response.

QUICK RECAP

- *Submodalities, the finer distinctions of the Modalities or Representational Systems, let us know how to interpret situations.*
- *By changing Submodalities, we can change our experience.*
- *Normally, the quickest way to use submodalities is to find the Driver ie the key Submodality that, when you change it, changes the others and makes the biggest difference to your experience. If you can't find your Driver, find the submodalities that do make a difference and change those so that your response is how you would like it to be.*
- *Eliciting and changing Submodalities is a quick process, because our unconscious mind works very quickly.*
- *Submodalities help you run your own brain. You can, for example, change how motivated you are to do something, how much you like something (eg foods), so that you can respond how you want to. Remember: who is driving your bus?*
- *Before making any change to your experience, do an Ecology check.*

CHAPTER 11

Gaining wisdom: as easy as 1-2-3

There is always more than one way to perceive a situation. You often hear people say that there are three sides to every argument – mine, yours and the 'truth' (whatever that may be), which is somewhere in between. As the ancient Native American saying goes, 'Walk a mile in another man's moccasins before you criticize him'.

In NLP there is a technique called Perceptual Positions, which essentially means putting yourself in someone else's moccasins, looking at a situation from different perspectives/positions so that you can perceive it in a different way and gain some insights or 'wisdom'. In my experience, there is no NLP technique more useful than this one.

WHY IS THE PERCEPTUAL POSITIONS TECHNIQUE SO USEFUL?

Perceptual Positions can be used in numerous ways. For example:

- To sell (products, services or persuade others of your ideas).

- To prevent and resolve conflicts and misunderstandings, either in a professional or personal context.

- To improve strategy, either for a department or an organisation, by seeing the points of view of other relevant and interested parties (shareholders, customers, employees, suppliers).

- To prepare for presentations, interviews and other meetings.

- To make decisions (the story goes that Andrew Carnegie, a Scot who made a fortune in America in the railway business, used the same principles as perceptual positions before making important decisions).

- To solve problems.

- To negotiate, whether in business, or your personal life (children and partners).

- To be creative (Walt Disney used a process similar to perceptual positions).

- To think what tactics or game-plan a sporting opponent may use.

- To coach, so that you can help your clients when they have any of the above situations.

✎ ACTION POINT

Think of some situations or relationships where you would benefit if you had greater insight into someone else's perspective. Keep these in the back of your mind as you read through this chapter. We will come back to this later.

WHAT ARE PERCEPTUAL POSITIONS?

Building on the point that there are three positions in an argument, there are three principle viewpoints in any situation:

- Mine, which we call position 1 or first position.

- Yours, which we call position 2 or second position. This is 'putting yourself in someone's moccasins'.

- A neutral observer's, which we call position 3 or third position. Often if we are asked to comment or advise on a situation that we are not involved with, we are able to see clearly and logically what those closely involved cannot see, and hence provide suggestions to progress the situation. Position 3 helps us to do this in our own situation.

Depending on the situation, we can introduce additional positions. For example, as indicated earlier, when using perceptual positions to make decisions, we could consider it from the perspective of all people, or groups of people, involved. The story goes that when Carnegie was faced with a difficult business decision, he would sit in the chairs of each of his board members to feel/see what it was like from their perspective, before coming to his decision. Similarly when developing a corporate strategy there are several relevant parties (such as employees, customers, suppliers, competitors and shareholders) whose perspectives you can consider.

HOW CAN WE USE PERCEPTUAL POSITIONS IN PRACTICE?

When using the perceptual positions techniques, essentially we consider the given situation from at least three perspectives, and take whatever insights we gain into account when taking future actions. Having identified a situation where it would be beneficial to have some insight, such as those mentioned above, we can then follow the process summarised in the exercise below.

1. Mark out three spaces on the floor, or three chairs, rather like the diagram below.

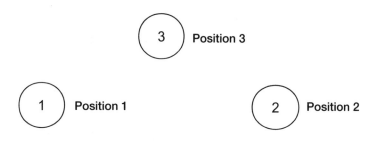

2. Stand/sit in position 1, as yourself, and ask yourself how you are feeling and what you are thinking as you face the person who you would like to understand better (ie position 2). Spend no more than a minute there.

3 Clear your mind and go to position 2, as the other person or group of people (eg the interviewer, the audience you're presenting to, the client(s), the person you are in 'conflict' with). As much as possible, adopt their physiology and posture, 'be' them as much as possible (remember the left hand side of the NLP Communication Model from Chapter 2 (p.19) – physiology impacts on state and internal representations), so by doing this you will be more likely to think like the other

person(s) and hence gain insights. Spend as much time as needed to gain insights into what they are thinking and feeling about the situation, as they look at 'that person' in position 1 (ie you).

4   Clear your mind and go and be in position 3, as a neutral observer/fly on the wall. Ask yourself (as the neutral observer) questions such as, 'what advice would I give both parties?', 'what do I notice about the situation that perhaps those two people haven't yet noticed?', 'what do they have in common/ what are their common aims?' or any other questions that are relevant to the specific scenario. It is important to be neutral, and at the same time to recognise that only the person in position 1 (ie you) can change as a direct result of this process. Make sure that position 3 is really dissociated from the other two positions, perhaps by making sure that position 3 is at the far end of the room. Spend as much time as needed to gain insights about the situation.

5. Take what you have learned from positions 2 and 3 and return to position 1, ie you. What are you going to do with this new knowledge, and by when?

6. Re-visit one or more of the positions again if you feel you would benefit from doing so, or even by create a fourth position somewhere further back from the three positions. Remember always to finish at position 1, so that you can incorporate what has been learned.

The diagram below summarises the process (the lines crossing the arrows represent a clearing of the mindset).

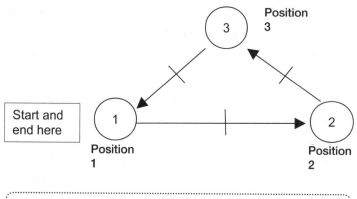

Where position 2 represents a group of people, for example another department with which your department is in conflict, pick someone who personifies that department for position 2.

TOP TIPS

Key points

- Spend only a few moments in position 1 – the reason you have not seen other perspectives is that you are already in position 1 and not able to dissociate from it sufficiently.

- Before moving to position 2, clear your mind by thinking of something neutral and unrelated, so that when you are in position 2, you can really think like that other person, **not** like you (in NLP terms, dissociate from yourself and associate into the other person.) Do the same before moving to position 3, so that you can be really neutral.

- Think/speak as the person in the position you are in. So, in position 2, say 'I' when you mean the interviewer/audience member/client, and in position 3 use 'he', 'she' and 'they' to mean the persons in position 1 and position 2.

- It is OK to visit the positions in any order as long as you start and end in position 1.

- If you are dealing with some form of 'conflict', make sure it is a relatively minor issue.

- And of course, as with all NLP techniques where you are changing your mindset, before you start the process do an ecology check and know what you want from the exercise.

🔍 EXAMPLE

Ingrid was a manager of a department of 40 to 50 people, and she had a difficult relationship with her boss (Sheila), who she felt was abrasive. In taking Ingrid through the perceptual positions exercise, when she got to position 2, she said (as Sheila), 'when I look at you Ingrid, I feel inadequate and threatened. You do such a great job managing this big department, and I feel that you'll get my job, so I keep you at a distance and make it a little difficult for you', and similar insightful comments that painted the situation in a completely different light to that which Ingrid had imagined. Then in position 3, as the neutral observer, she was able to notice various things about the relationship. A key one was that Ingrid and Sheila only ever spoke about work, and that it might be a good idea to have a chat over a coffee, outside work. The observer advised Ingrid to ask Sheila out for a coffee, which back in position 1, Ingrid agreed to do.

In subsequent sessions Ingrid told me that the relationship with Sheila had improved significantly.

In this example, it may have been completely obvious to everyone else what the situation was, and what Ingrid could have done about it. Had I 'recommended' that she asked Sheila for a coffee or something similar, Ingrid could have resisted, but having done the exercise she could not argue with her own advice.

Variations and other uses

The method outlined above is the standard way to do this in NLP, especially before the meeting, presentation, decision etc. It is perfectly possible to do the process in your head, perhaps while sitting in a meeting or negotiation (it would be a little strange to ask the interviewer or client if you could sit in their chair!). Clearly, you might not be saying to the other people what you are thinking as you do this, but you can put yourself in the other person's shoes during an interview or meeting, and also imagine how a neutral observer would advise you.

Some tips on using perceptual positioning

- In terms of creative thinking, Walt Disney apparently had different rooms for different types of thinking (creative, critic, realist). So when doing different types of thinking for your work you might want to use different rooms or physical spaces for different types of thinking, for example a specific meeting room for creative thinking and your boss' office for detailed planning. This can be linked to the principles of anchoring (ie stimulus-response) covered in the previous chapter, so that certain rooms can be linked to a certain type of thinking.

- For solving problems, position 1 could be the present problem situation, position 2 could be a point in the future when the problem had been resolved, and position 3 could be noticing which steps you took to solve the problem.

- To prepare for presentations, use positions 2 and 3 respectively to consider what the audience would want, and what a neutral observer would advise.

- Perceptual Positions can be used conversationally with other people. You could create position 2 thinking by asking, 'if Fred were here now, what would he be saying?', or 'If you were in Fred's shoes, what would you do?' Position 3 thinking could be created by asking, 'If you were advising Susan, who is in a similar situation to you, what advice would you give her?'

TOP TIPS

This latter point is extremely useful when coaching because clients often know the solutions to their problems, and when they themselves voice the solution, they cannot argue with it.

Making decisions

We can use perceptual positions to make decisions. For example, we can set up a position 2 for each of the main choices (2a, 2b etc) and spend time on each position, considering the outcome under both/all scenarios, before moving to position 3 and back to position 1.

ACTION POINT

Pick a situation from the earlier exercise on p.163, and use perceptual positions to gain insights and/or see a (different) way forward.

QUICK RECAP

- *Being able to put on the thinking hats of other people involved in situations and consider the wisdom of a neutral observer helps expand our thinking about situations, and creates ways forward.*
- *This type of thinking is probably one of the most useful ways to gain insights. If we were quickly able to see several other points of view, all of our relationship, not to mention our professional results, would be much better.*
- *As with all NLP techniques which change one's thinking, check the ecology before doing the process.*
- *When doing the perceptual positions exercise, make sure you step into the shoes and have the mindset of the relevant position (other person(s) and neutral observer).*
- *The ability to put oneself in other people's shoes, 'to walk in their moccasins', is an invaluable skill. Imagine the benefits if everyone were able to do it, if everyone were truly able to consider what the consequences of their actions would be on others.*

CHAPTER 12

Turning negatives into positives: reframing

An event is an event. The meaning we place on it, and therefore how we feel about it, is something that is more under our control than we might think. This chapter looks at how we can interpret events in ways that are useful to us. We will look at the technique of Reframing which allows us to put a positive spin on events, and turn apparent problems into opportunities.

REFRAMING

As you know from the Communication Model on p.20, we interpret events based on filters such as our beliefs and values. Therefore the meaning we place on an event depends on the filters we (unconsciously) use to interpret it. Another component determining the meaning of an event is the context in which it takes place. If we saw two men punching each other we might call the police, but if it happens in a boxing ring, that's fine. If we saw a man nodding and shaking his head from side to side and waving a short stick in seemingly random ways, we might question his sanity, but if he is standing in front of an orchestra in a theatre, we will probably admire and respect him.

So if the meaning of an event depends on the context in which it occurs and on the way we filter and interpret it, altering the context and/or the way we interpret it will alter the meaning. In NLP, the method of placing a more positive meaning on something is called Reframing.

Why is reframing so useful?

If we can consistently interpret events in our life in a positive way (putting a positive 'spin' on them), then the chances are that we will be happier and feel more positive. We can also use reframing to help others to do the same if we are coaching or managing them. Being able to turn 'problems' into 'opportunities' will also help improve results at work, and possibly change negative outlooks we have about certain situations into neutral or even positive ones.

Types of reframing

There are two main types of reframe – Context Reframes and Meaning Reframes (also known as Content Reframes.) We can reframe others as well as ourselves, and there will be some particular tips about how to reframe others later in the chapter. Let's take both types of reframe in turn.

Context reframes

A given behaviour may not be useful in one context, and may be neutral or even very useful in other contexts. A classic story often used in NLP to illustrate this relates to a father who drags his adolescent daughter into a psychotherapist's office, complaining that she is 'too headstrong'. The therapist pauses, and then says, 'Isn't it great that when she is older she will be able to stick up for herself in her relationships and in her career'. The context reframe was delivered by the therapist asking himself, '**where/ when would this behaviour be useful?**' (the behaviour of being headstrong, sticking up for yourself, not blindly doing what other people wanted you to do etc) and then delivering the reframe.

Examples of different contexts could be:

- **Time**: The word 'yet' can be used as a context reframe, because it changes the timeframe from 'now' to 'some point in the future'. Heavy snow on Christmas Day is welcomed in Northern Europe and North America; heavy snow at different times of the year is greeted somewhat differently.

- **Age**: Typical behaviours by 20 year olds (such as drinking and partying) would probably be considered strange or eccentric if a 70 year old did them.

- **Location**: Behaviour regarded as acceptable in a boxing ring has a different meaning in the street, and rain in the Sahara is probably greeted very differently from how it is greeted in London or New York.

- **Workplace/family/sport**: As with the 'headstrong daughter' example above, some acceptable behaviours at work or in sport would be unacceptable at home.

Meaning/content reframes

A Meaning/Content Reframe is when we consider that the event/situation has a different (more positive) meaning than the one we originally thought.

🔍 EXAMPLE

In 1996 I felt stuck in my finance role, and was offered an ideal job which unfortunately was between one and two hours 'drive away, depending on the traffic and the time I left home. Taking the train would have involved two 45 minute train journeys each way. I felt unsure about what to do. When discussing this with a friend, I felt very negatively about the train journey, and he said, 'At least you'll have a few hours to do the reading you'll have to do for your work'. This was like a light-bulb moment for me, and changed the 'travel problem' into a 'reading opportunity'. Fortunately, I was soon offered a big promotion at my existing role, which was 30 minutes away from home.

This example shows how meaning/content reframing works. The situation was unchanged, but the meaning I put on it had changed. We can create meaning reframes by asking ourselves, 'what else could this behaviour/situation mean or represent?', or 'what is it about the situation in this context that I (or the other person) hasn't yet noticed, that will bring about a different meaning and change my (or their) response and/or behaviour?'

To sum up:

- **Context reframes** consider the *same* behaviour in *different contexts* to change its meaning into a more positive one.

- **Meaning reframes** consider the *same* behaviour, and give it a *different meaning/interpretation* to change the meaning into a more positive one.

Making reframing work

We can reframe ourselves and we can reframe others. Sometimes it takes a little presence of mind to reframe ourselves, because when we are thinking negatively we sometimes cannot see other perspectives or meanings. The perceptual positions technique (see p.164) can be helpful here – we could imagine we are someone else, looking at it from their point of view (position 2) or that we are a neutral observer (position 3). In fact, perceptual positions is a form of context reframing.

If we want to reframe others it is important to make sure that we have 'permission' to reframe. It can be irritating if someone (no matter how well-meaning they may be) tries to help by putting a positive spin and you don't want them to do so (perhaps because it's not their place to do so or perhaps because it's not an appropriate time for it).

TOP TIPS

When someone is actually seeking, or is open to, help or advice in some way, and they are not emotionally charged about it, reframes are more likely to be successful than when the person is still upset.

Generally, reframes work best when:

- You are in rapport with the person. This links to the point above, and also, since the reframe can be a little cheeky sometimes, if you are not in rapport you can come across as being flippant.

  AND

- You have some knowledge of how the situation is a problem for the person concerned (so that you can relate the reframe more to the person's own interpretation of the situation rather than yours).

AND

- The reframe is plausible. In the examples above, it's totally plausible that the adolescent daughter would be able to stand up for herself, and that I could use the travel time to read.

AND

- The reframe is delivered congruently, ie that the person saying the reframe believes what they are saying.

Generally, the reframing phrase would start with words such as:

- 'Well, at least you can XXX (eg do some reading on the train)'

- 'Isn't it great that XXX (eg she'll be able to stand up for herself at work)'

- 'So now (at least) you'll be able to XXX'

- 'So at least you won't have to XXX'

- 'Thank goodness you're not XXX'

Here are some examples of reframes:

1. 'These exercises are boring.'

   Possible reframe: 'These exercises might be slow, but they will help me (you) get really fit and strong.' (This is a content/meaning reframe,ie, 'boring' becomes slow').

2. 'My boss doesn't appreciate me at all.'

   Possible reframe 1: 'Perhaps he/she trusts you enough to let you get on with it.' (This is a content/meaning reframe, ie, lack of appreciation become 'trust').

   Possible reframe 2: 'Perhaps your boss thinks you're strong-minded enough that you don't need constant praise.' (To do a content/meaning reframe, ie, change the interpretation 'doesn't appreciate me' into 'thinks you are strong-minded).

Possible reframe 3: 'At least you've got a job!'

3. 'My mother is always checking up on me.'

   Possible reframe: 'At least she loves you/cares for you. I bet many people wish their mother had shown that level of interest.' (This is a content/meaning reframe, ie, 'loves/cares' instead of 'checking up').

4. 'My team-mates never appreciate all the work I do.'

   Possible reframe: 'Will that matter when you've retired and you can look at all the trophies you've won?' (This is a context reframe ie, looking at trophies in the future).

TOP TIPS

- Generally, when reframing others, the first reframe that comes to mind with your 'positive spin' mindset will be the most effective.
- Beware of 'over-reframing'. Politicians are renowned for putting positive spins on events, and after a while the effect wears off and it can become annoying, and possibly lead to people not taking you seriously.
- As you will probably have realised, an effective way to do a content reframe is to redefine the word into a less negative or more positive word. In the examples above, 'boring' was redefined as 'slow', and 'checking up' was redefined as 'caring' or 'loving'.

ACTION POINT

Practise reframing for yourself any 'minor challenges' that you have. If appropriate, gently practise with others, bearing in mind the points made above.

QUICK RECAP

- *The meaning of virtually everything depends on the context we put it in.*
- *Reframing is the art of turning a negative into a neutral or a positive.*
- *Reframing is an extremely useful way to change the way we or someone else perceives a situation.*
- *There are two main types of Reframes – context, where we ask* when *or* where *else this would be useful, and Content/Meaning Reframes, where we ask* what *else this could mean.*
- *Remember, if you want to deliver effective Reframes ensure that you choose an appropriate time and place to do so, with an appropriate person with whom you are in Rapport, that the Reframe is plausible, and that you say it as if you believe it.*

PART 4

GAINING GREATER INSIGHT INTO YOURSELF AND OTHERS

PART 4

CHAPTER 13

Why people do what they do: values and motivation

As we covered in Chapter 2, Values are one of the filters within the Communication Model, and as we saw in Chapter 8, they are one of the more important aspects of the Logical Levels model.

In this chapter we will cover why values are so important, how to find out your and other people's values and how to use that information in a variety of situations.

VALUES AND MOTIVATION

From an NLP perspective, Values can be defined as 'what is important to us', or 'what we want or seek', in any particular context. For example, if one of our key values in a career context is 'intellectual stimulation', we will seek tasks and situations which stimulate us intellecutally. If one of our key values in the context of intimate relationships is 'sharing', we will seek a partner with whom we can share and who wants to share. If our values are not met, we may not feel as motivated or happy as when they are met.

As we mentioned earlier values will determine how we spend our time and direct our energies, because we tend to do things which are important to us and not do things which aren't important to us. They also strongly influence how we feel about what we have done afterwards. Many of us may regret some things we have done in our past because they 'go against the grain'.

Therefore, values are important aspects of our personality, as they drive our behaviours and motivate us towards what we want and away from what we don't want.

Values are context dependent: what is important to us in a career (for example *'challenge'*, *'learning new things'*, *'working with great people'*, *'making a difference'*, *'having a sense of achievement'*) will be different to what is important to us in a relationship, a house, or in a pair of shoes. Having said that, most people will have 'core values', values which apply in many contexts. For example, for me personally, *'integrity'* and *'honesty'* are core values, and I will want these values to be present in my career, in my relationships, in friendships and other key areas of my life.

Why learn about values?

A knowledge of values can be useful in numerous ways, for example:

- Managing and motivating people, both at work and in sport

- Recruiting

- Appraisals

- Team-building

- Making decisions, regarding anything from careers and partners, to which home to buy (see the example on p.188), and where to go on holiday

- Selling

- Having greater self-awareness and/or awareness of what is important to others

- Improving the level of satisfaction you have in your life

WHERE DO OUR VALUES COME FROM?

Our values come from our life experiences and are influenced by various factors including our upbringing, family, school, friends, economic circumstances, religious influences and the media. Our values can change and often do change as we mature and have different life experiences. Sometimes this can happen in moments. I remember that the attitudes of many of the guys I have worked with and played football with changed as soon as they knew their partner was pregnant. Being made redundant can also be a 'values-changing' experience.

USING VALUES: AN OVERVIEW

You can use the information on values in the chapter for yourself and other people. To work effectively with values, it is essential to know what is important to someone (or yourself), and ideally to have some idea of the relative importance of the things that are important. The best way to find out this information is simply to:

- Ask the right questions

  AND

- Listen to the answers

Typically, there are two main ways to elicit someone's values – formally and informally. You would use the formal method when you are coaching or doing appraisals, and the informal method when the situation is more conversational such as when selling. Both methods are similar.

We can find out what our values are in any or all of the main areas of our life, for example:

- Work, career, business, job
- Family
- Relationships
- Friends, social life
- Health and fitness
- Money and finances
- Personal development
- Spiritual development
- Religion
- Hobby

FINDING OUT YOUR VALUES

When eliciting your own values (or someone else's), choose a context (perhaps from the list on p.184) and then go through the following process. We will assume in the example below that you are finding out your own career values. For other contexts, simply substitute 'career' with the chosen context. You may want to ask a friend or colleague to help you by asking the questions and making a note of your answers, so that you can focus on simply answering. The following process is written for the person asking the questions.

Step 1: Standard questions.

Ask questions such as *'what's important to you in a career?'*, *'what do you want from your career?'*, and *'what do you look for from your career?'*

Make a note of what they say, *in their own words*. Do not suggest ideas as we want to find *their* values. We do not need them to explain why a value is important.

If they give us a phrase stated in the *negative*, such as, 'I don't want to be bored', ask, 'what do you want instead?'. They might say, 'variety', which is what you will write down.

If they give you a *behaviour* rather than a value, for example, 'having a tidy desk' or 'doing a good job', ask 'what's important to you about that?' or 'for what purpose?', so that you get a *value*.

Typically, people pause after about four to six values. Ask 'what else is important to you about your career?' and give them time to answer.

Step 2: Previous situations

Given that having our values met makes us feel motivated or happy, ask them to think of a specific time in their career when they felt really motivated (or happy), and what it was about that situation that caused them to feel so motivated/happy. Listen out for values (for example 'challenge', 'learning new things', 'working with great people', 'making a difference', 'having a sense of achievement') and if they have not mentioned them in step 1, ask if they are important and if so, add them to the list. If you are hearing lots of values that have not been mentioned in step 1, you could repeat step 2 for a different situation.

By this stage, you will typically have around 8–12 values.

Step 3: 'Catch-all'
Show them the list. Ask, 'if you had all this, what, if anything, would make you want to leave or say "No" to this career?' In other words, 'what, if anything, is missing?' Often there will be nothing missing. If there is something, add it to the list.

Step 4: Ranking
Although all the values on the list will be important, some will be more important than others. Ask the person to rank the values from 1 to 8 with 1 being the most important. Typically the top 4–6 values will provide the major amount of motivation in any given context, so continuing beyond 8 is normally of limited use. Another way of ranking, especially if there are 10 to 20 values, is to rank the absolutely essential values as 'A's, the important but not essential values as 'B's and the 'icing on the cake' values as 'C's. Sometimes it is useful to ask the person which of the two methods of ranking would be most beneficial to them.

Step 5: Check
As a 'check', offer the person two careers. One with ranked values of 5 to 8 (name them) (or the 'B's) and the second with ranked values of 1-4 (name them) (or the 'A's). The person should choose the second career, ie, the one with the most important values. If

they are unsure or choose the first one, revisit step 4 and ask them if they want to adjust the ranking.

> **TOP TIPS**
>
> With some contexts you may need to flex the questions slightly in steps 2, 3 and 5. For example, rather than asking, 'if you had all this in your *health and fitness*, what would make you want to leave it or say, "No?"', it is probably better to ask something like, 'is there anything missing from this list for it to be your ideal health and fitness situation/programme?'

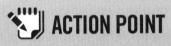

ACTION POINT

Use the questions above to discover your values in each of your main areas of life, so that you have a greater understanding of what drives you.

Once you have this information, you can use it in a variety of situations.

Making choices

If you want to make a choice between two careers, prospective partners, homes, or are looking to have a career, partner, home, you can use your values as a 'checklist' to see which one to choose, or which direction to take. You would look for a career/partner/home which met all your important values.

Q EXAMPLE

Nancy attended a seminar where I took people through the formal values elicitation process. She was looking for a committed relationship, and having done this exercise, she realised that the guy she had known for many years and with whom she had had an on-off relationship was actually the man for her – he ticked the main boxes. Within a week they were engaged, and they now have two beautiful daughters. Similarly, a couple attended my course having been looking for a new home for six months. They did the values exercise on 'house', and within a week had found their ideal home because they knew what they were looking for.

Selling

When selling, if you know what your prospective customer is looking for from a consultant/lawyer/house/pair of shoes, or whatever you are selling, *and* you are able to deliver what they want, then you would really be serving them by selling them your product or service. Please read the section on *Eliciting values informally* (p.190) to note how to flex the values elicitation questions when selling.

Interviews

Similarly when promoting yourself at an interview, if you know what the prospective employer is looking for and you can demonstrate that you have the desired qualities, it will give you a better chance of success. Linked to that, if you know your own values you can ask questions to find out whether your values will be met by the role. Interviewers generally think highly of candidates who ask searching questions to ascertain whether the role is suitable for them.

Recruiting

When recruiting, if you profile the job in terms of values (as well as competencies), you can ask the candidate relevant questions and select someone who has a suitable motivation, and who will fit into the team. For example, if you identify that you want to recruit an employee for whom challenge, professionalism, learning and being part of a great team are important, you can mention this in the job advert and elicit the candidate's values at the interview to see if there is a match.

Managing people

As a manager, if you know about your staff's values your job becomes a lot easier. You simply need to offer them the opportunity to have more of their values and they will be motivated. In order to find out this information from staff at appraisals, managers may need to 'pre-frame' (ie set up) the conversation along the following lines:

'As your manager, I want you to be really happy and fulfilled in your work, because it benefits me, you, the company/organisation and our customers/clients/patients. In order for me to help you be happy, it would really help if you told me what was important to you in your work so that I can help you have more of what you want and less of what you don't want. I can't promise I will be able to do all of this, but I do promise that I will do everything I realistically can within the organisational and departmental constraints to help you have more of what you want. Are you willing to do this? If so, there are some questions I'd like to ask you.'

Please note. It is *essential* that you *keep your word* if you do this as a manager. Of course, you probably cannot double their salary, give them a massive promotion or treat them advantageously compared to other members of the team. You can however be flexible and go out of your way to help them within the confines of your role. When your employees see you do this, they will almost certainly go that extra mile.

Gaining greater satisfaction and improving situations

One final way to use information on values for yourself, or when coaching/managing others, is to improve your level of satisfaction in any given area. Knowing your values in a given context, you could rank on a scale of 0–10 the extent to which each of your top values are being met. For example, if your most important value is 'challenge' and it is being fulfilled 7 out of 10, you could ask yourself, 'what would take the score to an 8, 9 or even 10?' Do the same for the other top values.

When using values to make choices or to sell, concentrate on making sure the most important values are met.

You may be wondering, 'what do some of these values (eg challenge) actually mean?' because they mean different things to different people. That's a great question – hold that thought and we will cover it later this chapter.

ELICITING VALUES INFORMALLY

If you would like to elicit values in a conversational or informal setting, such as in a selling situation, you can find out someone's values in one of two ways.

Firstly just listen and use your sensory acuity. Because values are like 'hot buttons' of motivation, people will often indicate to you non-verbally when something is important, perhaps by a subtle shift in body posture, or by emphasising it with their voice. For example, 'the last consultant we had was not reliable at all. And he didn't get on with people. The one before that was great, very creative in his thinking, always delivered what he said and made a real difference to our business.'

The other way is to casually ask the elicitation questions, perhaps having asked a question such as, 'can I ask some questions that would help us both?' For example, if you are selling consultancy services to a business, you could ask questions like:

1. 'What do you look for from a firm of consultants?', and/or

   'Have you ever worked with a firm of consultants that you were happy with? What was it about them that made you happy?'

2. 'If you had all this (mention what they have told you) in a firm of consultants, would that be enough or is there anything else that is really important to you?'

3. 'Which of these are most important?' (Get the top four or five. It is probably not appropriate to do the 'check' mentioned on p.186).

Then, assuming you could demonstrate that you could meet what the client is looking for (especially the really important ones), show and explain to them how your services/products meet their needs.

FINDING OUT WHAT VALUES MEAN

As a manager, if a member of your team tells you that 'challenge' is important to them in their work, that is helpful, and you may not know what *they* mean by 'challenge' (you'll know what *you* mean by 'challenge). If you know specifically what they mean by 'challenge' you will have far more of an idea about what to do to motivate them (or what not to do to avoid de-motivating them). The same principles apply when selling (knowing specifically what prospects actually want) and job-seeking/making decisions (knowing exactly what you are looking for and asking relevant questions at the interview).

There are some useful questions that can help you find out what values mean in situations where you are using values. Using 'challenge' as an example:

- 'What has to happen for you to know that you are challenged/ have a challenge?'

- 'How do you know when you're challenged?'

- 'What does challenge mean to you?'

- 'How do you know when someone/something challenges you?'

- 'What is your evidence procedure for challenge?'

- 'What causes you to feel challenged?'

- 'What would have to happen for you to feel not challenged?'

Normally you would use just one or two of these questions for each value.

ACTION POINT

Regularly (perhaps annually) review your values from each of your key areas of life, elicit your values and what they mean, (or review previous results and amend the list), and set at least one well-formed goal in each area of life that is in line with your values (ie will give you more of the higher-ranked values in that area of life). This exercise will take around four hours a year. Write down your answers. If you do this exercise, and keep in mind the mindset for success, the Principles for Success and the well-formed conditions for goals, it is probably *the* most important and beneficial four hours you will spend each year.

QUICK RECAP

- *Values are incredibly important filters. They provide our drive and motivation, and can act as a way for us to evaluate what we have done.*
- *Everyone has values, even if they are completely different to yours.*
- *Values change and evolve over time.*
- *Values are context dependant (careers, relationships, buying shoes).*
- *In any context, there will normally be a 'hierarchy' of values – some values will be more important than others.*
- *Knowing your own values in different contexts will help you make better decisions, and can help you increase your level of satisfaction in that context and in your life generally.*
- *Knowing and understanding the values of your staff, and what these values mean, will almost certainly make you a more effective manager.*
- *Regularly review your values in the key areas of your life.*
- *Make sure that the goals you set will give you more of what's important to you.*

CHAPTER 14

Understanding and influencing behaviour: deep filters

Meta Programmes is NLP jargon for a set of filters which sit beyond, or underpin, other filters. They are deeply embedded filters, and for this reason we will refer to them as deep filters. These deep filters are key components of our personality, and they, along with values, determine our responses to many situations, and also relate to our 'preferences' for dealing with and presenting information.

An awareness of deep filters is an extremely useful tool when dealing with people; if you communicate in a way that is complementary to someone's deep filters (ie preferences) you will have a much better chance of influencing them.

In this chapter we will be covering five key deep filters and how to use these deep filters to communicate effectively.

WHY ARE DEEP FILTERS SO USEFUL?

Deep filters are useful in the following areas:

- Recruiting suitable people for a role

- Selling, to help present information to meet buyers' preferences

- Team-building, to ensure you have an appropriate mix

- Advertising

- Motivating people, whether as a manager or sports coach

- Creating a better awareness and understanding of ourselves and others, to enhance relationships

- General communication

FIVE KEY DEEP FILTERS

Although there are around 15–20 key deep filters we will be concentrating on five which are particularly useful. All five are on a spectrum, ie there are two extremes of response, with many people being somewhere in between the two ends of the spectrum. For each of the five we will cover the following:

- A brief explanation of the filter, and the two ends of the spectrum for that filter

- How to recognise the patterns of behaviour at both ends of the spectrum by noticing their behaviour and/or listening to their language

- Some tips regarding how to influence the person depending on where they are on the spectrum

There is no right or wrong, nor a good or bad place to be on any deep filter spectrum. Whatever someone's deep filters are, they are useful in some contexts and may not be so useful in other contexts. Like values, meta programmes/deep filters are context specific, so someone's preferences at home may be different from those at work.

It is useful to be aware of our own deep filters so that we know how we operate and can build more flexibility if we desire. We often deal with and treat others the way we would like to be dealt with ourselves, so a knowledge of our own filters can help us be aware of this, and therefore respond to others according to *their* preferences, not *ours*.

The five deep filters that we are going to cover are:

1. The direction filter – Towards/Away From

2. The reason filter – Options/Procedures

3. The frame of reference filter – Internal/External

4. The relationship filter – Sameness/Differences

5. The chunk size filter – Big Picture/Detail

Towards or *away from*

Some people are very focused on, and motivated by, what they want to achieve, and the benefits they would get from achieving their goal. Other people tend to pay more attention to the obstacles that they perceive are in their way, and they may even be motivated by the chance to fix or solve problems.

These are the two ends of the deep filter known as the 'direction filter'. It is commonly referred to as 'carrot or stick' motivation; some people are motivated by the 'carrot' ie they want to move *towards* what they want to have, and other people are motivated by the 'stick' ie they move *away from* what they don't want to happen.

For example, one member of a sports team may be motivated to win because they like winning and it gives them a sense of achievement and satisfaction, whereas another team member may be motivated to win because they don't want to lose and don't want to play badly. Both may have an equal degree of motivation, yet the first has *towards* motivation, and the second has *away from* motivation. These are examples of the two ends of the spectrum. Other team members may be motivated by a combination of *towards* and *away from* motivation.

Tips for recognising *towards* and *away from*

Here are some indicators for either end of the spectrum. People may have a combination of these, which will indicate roughly where they are on the spectrum. Generally, people who are *towards* motivated will tend to:

- Stay focused on their goal

- Be energised by the opportunity to achieve goals ('if you train hard you'll have a good chance of being picked for the team')

- Use words and phrases such as 'achieve', 'get', 'have', 'win', 'targets', 'what we want is XXX', and 'objectives', especially when talking about *what* is important to them and *why* something is important to them.

They may also not be aware of potential problems or pitfalls, because they are highly focused on what they want to have.

Generally people who are *away from* motivated will tend to:

- Notice what is wrong with a situation and the problems to be avoided

- Be motivated by solving or fixing problems

- Be motivated by deadlines (as opposed to target dates), and if they may lose out on something if they don't do a particular thing ('if you don't train hard you probably won't get picked for the team').

- Use words and phrases which mention what situations they would avoid, get rid of, not have, undesired situations, problems, negations, or words indicating necessity like 'have to', 'must', 'should', 'ought to', especially when talking about what is important to them and why something is important to them.

They may have trouble focusing on goals and prioritising, because whatever is wrong will attract their attention.

Tips for using *towards* and *away from*

In terms of influencing people it is probably more beneficial to use *towards* language and motivation for those who are predominantly *towards* motivated, and *away from* language and motivation for those who are predominantly *away from* motivated. Where people are either in the middle, or if you are not sure, or if you are speaking to a group of people, then use a combination. For example, if you are addressing a mixed audience of colleagues you might say something like, 'and by being flexible, we can win contracts and achieve our targets. If we fail to adjust to changes in the industry, we will fall behind our competitors and lose market share.'

By using appropriate influencing language you will have the best chance of motivating people, and minimise the chances of switching them off. (In case you didn't notice, there was a *towards* and an *away from* statement in that last sentence.)

Options or *procedures*

Some people are motivated by the prospect of finding new or other ways to do tasks/activities whilst others prefer to follow established procedures. These two ends of the 'reason filter' spectrum are known as *options* and *procedures*. This filter is particularly useful when managing and recruiting, as certain jobs are more suitable for those with an *options* preference whilst other jobs are more suited to those with a *procedures* preference.

Tips for recognising *options* and *procedures*

Here are some indicators for either end of the spectrum. People may have a combination of these which will indicate roughly where they are on the spectrum.

Generally people who have an *options* preference will tend to:

- Look for new or better ways of doing something, because they believe there's always a better or newer way

- Dislike sticking to routines for prolonged periods of time, although they may like creating procedures for others to follow

- Seek to 'bend the rules', be flexible or look for ways to improve procedures

- Like to have different options to consider

If you ask them why they chose their current work, they will use words that indicate values, (such as the 'chance to achieve', 'fulfilment', 'challenge', 'working with great people'), or indicate that there was choice, options and opportunities.

Generally, people who have a *procedures* preference will tend to:

- Feel happier following the rules and guidelines

- Believe there is a 'right' way to do something, according to the tried and tested way, and hence want fewer alternatives to consider than someone with an *options* preference (at an extreme, they may want only one 'choice')

If you ask them why they chose their current work, they will tend to tell you *how* it happened, in other words give you the story or procedure.

Tips for using *options* and *procedures*

In terms of using this filter, *generally* we would want people with a significant amount of *options* preference in more senior and creative jobs, where flexibility, creativity and generally the ability to think out of the box is important. *Generally* we would want people with a significant amount of *procedures* preference in less senior roles, and roles that require lots of repetition. I would want the mechanic servicing my brakes to be *procedures* – I'd want him to follow the right, tried and tested procedure, every time.

When selling, be willing to be more flexible with *options* prospects than you would with *procedures* prospects. As a sports coach, be more creative with the training sessions for *options* athletes than you would for *procedures* athletes.

The opportunities and options to use these deep filters are endless – I'm sure you can think of alternatives yourself. In order to have the best chance of using deep filters in the right way, the way that has been tried and tested, just follow the procedures for eliciting and using these filters. (Did you spot the *options* and *procedures* statements in the previous two sentences?)

Internal or *external* reference

This deep filter is about how we find motivation; is it from external sources, or from internal standards and beliefs? The two ends of the 'frame of reference filter' spectrum are known as '*internally referenced*' and '*externally referenced*'. This filter is particularly useful when recruiting and managing people.

Tips for recognising *internal* and *external*

Here are some indicators for either end of the spectrum. People may have a combination of these which will indicate roughly where they are on the spectrum. Generally people who have an *internally referenced* preference will tend to:

- Set their own standards and decide for themselves the quality of their work and other people's work

- Take advice only from people who *they* believe are competent

- Be self-motivated.

When asked how they know that they have done a good job, they will indicate that they know based on their own assessment and criteria.

Generally people who have an *externally referenced* preference will tend to:

- Need other people's opinions, direction and feedback

- Accept and seek advice from people without necessarily qualifying whether the person is knowledgeable on the subject

When asked how they know that they have done a good job, they will indicate that they know based on other people's assessment, criteria and feedback.

Tips for using *internal* and *external*

In terms of how to influence people you could use some of the following words and phrases with *internally referenced* people: 'only you can decide', 'you know it's your choice', 'what do you think?', 'you may want to consider...', 'here is a suggestion for you to think about'.

To influence *externally referenced* people often it is enough to mention what other people will say or think, or what a particular person (or magazine/newspaper) has said.

Generally, with *internally referenced* people, you might want to give them the opportunity to comment early in a project. If not, and they don't agree with the way the project is being done, they may be disruptive. Also, when managing *internally referenced* people, you might want to check regularly that they are on track and doing what *you* want them to do, as opposed to what *they* want to do. If you are a manager, think about how much feedback you give people. When managing *externally referenced* people, make sure you give them plenty of feedback – a yearly appraisal is nowhere near enough.

TOP TIPS

When presenting to a group of people for the first time, because there will be a number of people with a significant amount of *internal reference*, make sure you establish credibility by mentioning some of your background and relevant achievements. Remember, internally referenced people decide for themselves who they listen to, so make sure you establish credibility and give them reasons to listen to you.

Only you can know how you will use deep filters in your life. On the other hand, if you want to know how some other people have used them, please see the *References and further reading* section (p.239). (You probably spotted the phrase for *internally referenced* people and the subsequent one for *externally referenced* people.)

Sameness or difference

This deep filter is about how we react to change, and how much change we like and feel comfortable with. Do we prefer things to stay the same (*sameness*) or do we want lots of change (*difference*)?

Tips for recognising sameness and difference
Here are some indicators for either end of the 'relationship filter' spectrum. Generally people who have a *sameness* preference will tend to:

- Like things to stay the same, and feel uncomfortable with big or frequent changes

- Seek change only very rarely, for example, they may seek to change jobs only once every 15–25 years

- Notice how things are similar to what they know

Generally people who have a *difference* preference will tend to:

- Want and seek constant, significant or frequent change (every year or two), and get bored if things stay the same

- Notice differences and changes in situations

We can conversationally find out where someone is on the spectrum (in the context of work) by asking, 'what's the relationship between what you're doing this year and last year?', or you could ask, 'how often do you change jobs?'. *Sameness* people will notice and mention how things are the same as they were, or that they change jobs roughly every 15–25 years. *Difference* people will notice and mention how things are different, and typically change jobs or roles every two years. Combinations indicate where someone is on the spectrum.

Tips for using *sameness* and *difference*

When managing *sameness* people, especially if there are changes happening in the workplace, do as much as possible to keep things the same, or at least highlight the similarities. When managing *difference* people, make sure they have sufficient change (assuming you want them to stay), and even consider creating change for them (for example, switching their office or changing the accounts they manage).

You may occasionally find that people with a strong *difference* preference frequently disagree or do the opposite of what you ask for (parents of teenagers probably know this type of behaviour well!). If you find that someone is doing that type of behaviour (in NLP we call them 'mis-matchers'), one thing you can do is ask them to do the opposite of what you want, or say, 'I don't suppose you'll be able to do XXX (the thing you want them to do)', or 'I'm not sure if you'll agree with this' if you want them to agree with you.

With the other deep filters we have covered, according to research reported in *Words That Change Minds* (Kendall/Hunt, 1995), Shelle Rose Charvet's excellent book on deep filters, the spread of people along the spectrum is roughly even. However, for this filter, most people are closer to the *sameness* end of the spectrum. This explains why there are relatively few people who always buy the latest brand new technology (*difference*), and that most people prefer remaining with their existing product and take their time until the new product is established (*sameness*). For those of you working in advertising or marketing, think about who you want to target, and the words you are using. Words such as 'new', 'brand new', 'unrecognisable' or 'transforms' will attract the relatively few *differences* people, whereas words such as 'improved' and 'washes even whiter' will attract people closer to the *sameness* end of the spectrum.

You might be looking forward to using these deep filters, and indeed all the information in this book, to help transform how you operate. Other readers will use this information to improve gradually, (or perhaps, very gradually) how you communicate with people (*difference* and then *sameness* statements).

Big picture or *detail*

This deep filter relates to the Hierarchy of Ideas covered in Chapter 7 (p.93). It is about what size chunks of information people process comfortably – do they want small chunks, or do they prefer big concepts?

The kind of language that you hear *big picture* people use, and which you can use when influencing them, are words like 'in essence', 'conceptually', 'overall', 'generally', 'in summary', 'the big picture', 'in a nutshell' and 'essentially'.

The kind of language that you hear *detail* people use, and which you can use when influencing them, are words like 'precise(ly)', 'specific(ally)', 'exact(ly)' and you will normally find that they will provide lots of detail or get into the 'nitty gritty' and enjoy it.

You may wish to make your own summary of this section. To obtain even more information about how to use this material, or to learn more detail about the deep filters briefly mentioned, refer to the *References and further reading* section. (Did you notice the *big picture*, then *detail* statements?)

ACTION POINT

With your knowledge of these five deep filters, spend a few moments considering where you are on the spectrum of each one. Do this for the main 'contexts' in your life (eg work, home, sport). This is an art – it may be useful to refine where you think you are, and remember these deep filters are context dependent, so your responses at work may be different in different areas of your life. You may also want to reflect on the deep filter profiles of other people in your life.

Q EXAMPLE

I was coaching a managing director a few years ago. She was having some 'challenges' managing her staff. I found out her deep filters, explained the traits of the different ends of the spectrum, and we discussed what she thought the traits of her staff were. She could clearly identify why there were challenges, mainly due to her being at opposite ends of the spectrum from her staff for some of the filter patterns. At the end of the session, she said that she wished she had known about these filters 20 years ago – it would have helped her career significantly.

Appendix B (p.231) provides a summary of the keys traits and influencing language of the deep filters covered in this chapter.

APPLICATIONS OF DEEP FILTERS

We can use deep filters in several ways. When doing a job specification when recruiting, consider the main deep filters that will be relevant and then look for that trait in applicants. When selling, find out the buyers' deep filters and present your offering accordingly. Do they want you to present options, or is there a 'right way' to do it? And if buyers are *internally referenced*, make sure you establish credibility and use *internal* influencing language.

When speaking to or communicating with groups, consider the likely profile of the audience and communicate accordingly (if you are not sure, use a combination). For example, I would expect an audience of senior executives to have a significant amount of *towards*, *options* and *big picture*.

When planning your career, consider your own deep filter profile (from the exercise above), and the types of filters that would be required for a particular role. Is there an acceptable match?

If there is a communication 'issue' it may be that there is a mismatch of deep filters. By understanding these filters you can be more tolerant, and even make changes to your natural way of behaving, for example providing lots of feedback to an *externally referenced* employee, even though you may be very *internally referenced*.

🔍 EXAMPLE

I have a friend who is highly qualified and proficient in NLP. He is highly options, and big picture and his business partner, also highly trained in NLP, is highly procedures and relatively detail. Because they know this, if his partner starts to tell the whole story, he politely asks her to fast-forward to the end. Similarly, if he just gives a quick summary and doesn't say how he wants something, she politely asks him to give more detail about what he wants. It is done respectfully, and they manage to accommodate their different styles and preferences and be a really effective team.

The *References and further reading* section has some pointers if you would like to find out more about these and other deep filters.

QUICK RECAP

- *Deep Filters are fundamental aspects of our personality and explain why we do things and behave the way we do.*
- *There are around 15–20 of these filters, and a knowledge of them will help us to understand how to predict and influence behaviour in a variety of contexts.*
- *The five key Deep Filters are:*
  1. *The direction filter – Towards/Away From*
  2. *The reason filter – Options/Procedures*
  3. *The frame of reference filter – Internal/External*
  4. *The relationship filter – Sameness/Differences*
  5. *The chunk size filter – Big Picture/Detail*
- *For each of the five filters we covered there is a spectrum of responses – relatively few people are at the extremes of the spectrum.*
- *For each filter, people give indications of where they are on the spectrum via their behaviours and their language.*
- *Remember, everyone is different. To get the best out of people, treat them according to their preferences, not yours. Remember too that Deep Filters may vary in different contexts.*

CHAPTER 15

Quickstart guide: summary of key points

Chapter 1 What is NLP?

- NLP provides a set of powerful tools to help you to change the way you think and give you the edge in certain situations, so that you can have more of what you want and less of what you don't want.

- It can be used in numerous situations and different areas of life.

- It helps people to communicate more effectively, change behaviours and beliefs, and to 'model' or replicate excellence more consistently and in other situations.

- It is **not** a substitute for appropriate medical or therapeutic treatment.

- It is used most effectively when seeking win-win situations.

Chapter 2 Communication: What happens inside our mind?

- We all filter out externally generated information to provide ourselves with an Internal Representation, or rather an 'internal *re*-presentation' of what we think we have experienced through our five senses.

- The key filter processes are Deletion, Distortion and Generalisation, based on our language, beliefs, values, attitudes, experiences and deep filters.

- Given that we all filter differently, it's useful for us to understand what Internal Representations other people may have formed from our communication, so that we can adjust our approach and communication accordingly.

- It is also useful to accept that we do not always make useful Internal Representations from other people's communications. By being aware of this, we can begin to examine our responses, and use some of the NLP skills available to seek alternative ways to respond.

Chapter 3 The mindset for success: the fundamental attitudes within NLP

- Operate from the Principles for Success.

- Always start with the goal in mind.

- Notice whether you're on track to get the results you want.

- Be flexible enough to change if you are not on track.

- Take action!

- Learn and operate from the NLP Presuppositions – they work.

- Notice when you are 'at cause' and 'at effect'. If ever you are 'at effect', ask yourself how you can move to being 'at cause'.

Chapter 4 Your goals: how to set and achieve them

- Setting goals is an essential part of achieving what you want. It is one of the Principles for Success. By knowing what you want and setting goals appropriately, you are far more likely to achieve your goal and avoid wasting time striving for goals which are not right for you.

- Set different types of goals – outcome (big picture and/or long-term), performance (what you are going to do and/or medium-term) and process (how you are going to do it and/or short-term) goals, using the principles outlined in this chapter.

- Pay particular attention to whether the goal is ecological (ie right for you and the people around you), and whether by achieving it you will have more choice, options and subsequent benefits just from achieving this one goal.

- Set goals for each of the main areas of your life, such as career, family, health/fitness and finances, so that you can takes steps to have the kind of life you want.

- Review your goals regularly. Do they need tweaking or updating in the light of new circumstances?

- Once you have achieved your goal, set new goals when the time is right for you to do so.

Chapter 5 Getting people on your side: how to build trust with anyone

- A significant amount of communication is done non-verbally, via physiology and voice tonality.

- The ability to notice subtle changes in people's physiology and voice tonality is called Sensory Acuity.

- When Calibrating, you are comparing one person to themself, not to others.

- Practise developing your Sensory Acuity skills. It will help you build Rapport with people.

- Being able to build Rapport with people is essential to any good relationship.

- Build Rapport with people by Matching or Mirroring their body language (especially posture, gestures and breathing) and/

or voice tonality (especially volume and speed of speech) for a period of time (called Pacing). Do so subtly, out of conscious awareness. If you make it too obvious, people will know you have been reading about NLP! Remember, a little goes a long way.

Chapter 6 How to speak everyone's language: becoming quad-lingual

- There are five Representational Systems (Visual, Auditory, Kinaesthetic, Olfactory and Gustatory) plus Auditory Digital.

- Remember that we use all of the Representational Systems, and that many of us have a preferred system.

- We can use our knowledge of Representational Systems and Predicates to build Rapport and communicate more effectively with individuals and groups.

- There are various indicators of the Preferred Representational System that someone has., such as how quickly they speak, the words they use, or the hobbies or work they choose.

- The more flexible we can be with using different Predicates the more we will speak the four different languages in English.

- Watching peoples' eye patterns can give us an indication of which Representational System someone is using at a given moment.

Chapter 7 Using language to influence: choosing your words for maximum impact

- Language is a very important topic, and the benefits of practising using the language patterns and tips shown in this chapter are immense.

- Language can be abstract or detailed, and the questions covered in the Hierarchy of Ideas help us to gain greater levels of abstraction (Chunking up), greater levels of details (Chunking down) or to think laterally.

• Remember, we all use the language patterns mentioned in this chapter anyway. The purpose of this chapter is to help you be even more aware of them than you have already been.

• We all use the language of Distortions, Deletions and Generalisations, and we can probe or question other people's language to uncover unspoken meaning.

• When questioning and using the Hierarchy of Ideas and The Meta Model, please remember to use common sense, make sure you are in Rapport, and resist any possible temptation to 'do NLP *to* someone'.

Chapter 8 Being true to yourself: alignment

• The Logical Levels model has six levels – purpose/mission, identity, beliefs and values, capabilities, behaviours and environment.

• It is an extremely useful model to help us structure our thinking, and gain increased personal or organisational alignment.

• The model can be used as a guide to problem-solving, by looking at which level(s) the problem arises and then dealing with it at either that level or a higher one. Similarly, possible solutions can be evaluated by using this model.

• It can also be used as a way to make changes or decisions.

• The model can be used to become even better as a manager, leader or coach.

• Generally, ask for changes to be made at *behavioural* level when giving feedback to individuals.

Chapter 9 How to be in *the* right State: managing your emotions

- Setting Anchors is a simple and very effective way to manage your emotional State in many potentially challenging situations such as interviews, presentations, meetings and important sports competitions.

- Remember the ITURN (Intensity, Timing, Uniqueness, Replicability, Number) mnemonic when setting Anchors.

- Following the seven steps to Anchoring process outlined will help you create long-lasting Anchors.

- Mentally rehearsing an event beforehand will improve your chances of success. Do Dissociated and/or associated mental rehearsal, using several likely scenarios, with each scenario turning out the way you want it to.

- Remember to top up the anchor, especially when something great happens to you.

Chapter 10 How to really use your brain: changing your responses to situations

- Submodalities, the finer distinctions of the Modalities or Representational Systems, let us know how to interpret situations.

- By changing Submodalities, we can change our experience.

- Normally, the quickest way to use submodalities is to find the Driver, ie the key submodality that, when you change it, changes the others and makes the biggest difference to your experience. If you can't find your Driver, find the Submodalities that do make a difference and change those so that your response is how you would like it to be.

- Eliciting and changing Submodalities is a quick process, because our unconscious mind works very quickly.

- Submodalities help you run your own brain. You can, for example, change how motivated you are to do something, how much you like something (eg foods), so that you can respond how you want to. Remember: who is driving your bus?

- Before making any change to your experience, do an Ecology check.

Chapter 11 Gaining wisdom: as easy as 1-2-3

- Being able to put on the thinking hats of other people involved in situations and consider the wisdom of a neutral observer helps expand our thinking about situations, and creates ways forward.

- This type of thinking is probably one of the most useful ways to gain insights. If we were quickly able to see several other points of view, all of our relationships, not to mention our professional results, would be much better.

- As with all NLP techniques which change one's thinking, check the Ecology before doing the process.

- When doing this exercise, make sure you step into the shoes and have the mindset of the relevant position (other person(s) and neutral observer).

- The ability to put oneself in other people's shoes, 'to walk in their moccasins', is an invaluable skill. Imagine the benefits if everyone were able to do it, if everyone were truly able to consider what the consequences of their actions would be on others.

Chapter 12 Turning negatives into positives: Reframing

- The meaning of virtually everything depends on the context we put it in.

- Reframing is the art of turning a negative into a neutral or a positive.

- Reframing is an extremely useful way to change the way we or someone else perceives a situation.

- There are two main types of Reframes – context, where we ask *when* or *where* else this would be useful, and Content/Meaning reframes, where we ask *what* else this could mean.

- Remember, if you want to deliver effective Reframes ensure that you choose an appropriate time and place to do so, with an appropriate person with whom you are in Rapport, that the Reframe is plausible, and that you say it as if you believe it.

Chapter 13 Why people do what they do: values and motivation

- Values are incredibly important filters. They provide our drive and motivation, and can act as a way for us to evaluate what we have done.

- Everyone has values, even if they are completely different to yours.

- Values change and evolve over time.

- Values are context dependant (careers, relationships, buying shoes).

- In any context, there will normally be a 'hierarchy' of values – some values will be more important than others.

- Knowing your own values in different contexts will help you make better decisions, and can help you increase your level of satisfaction in that context and in your life generally.

- Knowing and understanding the values of your staff, and what these values mean, will almost certainly make you a more effective manager.

- Regularly review your values in the key areas of your life.

- Make sure that the goals you set will give you more of what's important to you.

Chapter 14 Understanding and influencing behaviour: deep filters

- Deep filters are fundamental aspects of our personality and explain why we do things and behave the way we do.

- There are around 15–20 of these filters, and a knowledge of them will help us to understand how to predict and influence behaviour in a variety of contexts.

- The five key deep filters are:

  1. The direction filter – Towards/Away From

  2. The reason filter – Options/Procedures

  3. The frame of reference filter – Internal/External

  4. The relationship filter – Sameness/Differences

  5. The chunk size filter – Big Picture/Detail

- For each of the five filters we covered there is a spectrum of responses – relatively few people are at the extremes of the spectrum.

- For each filter, people give indications of where they are on the spectrum via their behaviours and their language.

- Remember, everyone is different. To get the best out of people, treat them according to their preferences, not yours.

CHAPTER 16

Using NLP in daily life

Throughout this book, we have taken a given topic and looked at how it can be used in various different contexts and situations. In this chapter we will be doing the opposite, in other words taking situations and contexts and asking which NLP techniques could be useful.

The explanations will be kept to a minimum, since you have read the book and can refer to any particular parts as necessary.

There are numerous contexts and situations where NLP can be applied. The main ones that are considered here are as follows:

- The workplace
- Coaching
- Sport
- Relationships

This chapter considers the main NLP techniques that are particularly relevant in each area. The following principles are fundamental to each area and will not be specifically referred to in the four areas mentioned above:

- The NLP Communication Model
- The Presuppositions of NLP
- Being 'at cause' and taking responsibility for your results

- The Principles for Success

- Ecology

- Sensory acuity

- Rapport

- Representational systems and predicates

- The Meta Model questions (asking questions to clarify what people mean)

Much of the following information is in bullet point form, since you will have read about the relevant techniques and already have a good grasp of how to apply them. Please note that just because a technique is not mentioned below it does not mean it is not useful, nor does it mean that they all have to be used. Use whichever techniques are useful.

NLP IN THE WORKPLACE

We will consider several situations that occur in the workplace and the main NLP techniques that would be useful.

Managing people
- Perceptual positions: to see the world from the staff's point of view.

- Hierarchy of Ideas: to know which level to pitch information at.

- Deep filters: to communicate in the way staff prefer and match their preferences.

- Well-formed outcomes: for career planning, appraisals and team goals.

- Values: to assist in motivating staff and avoiding de-motivating them.

Appraisals

- Submodalities: to ensure your own internal representations are positive before the meeting.

- Resource anchoring: especially if you are the staff member in the appraisal.

- Perceptual positions: to see the world from the point of view of the person you are appraising or who is appraising you.

- Hierarchy of Ideas: for knowing which level to pitch information at.

- Values: to find out what is important to the staff member, as well as finding out what the individual values mean.

- Logical Levels: to find ways to make performance even better.

- Well-formed outcomes: to set targets for the next year.

Conflict prevention and resolution

- Perceptual positions: to see both perspectives, and to help each party see the other's perspective.

- Hierarchy of Ideas: chunking upwards to gain agreement, and then chunking downwards slowly to agree the details.

Selling

- Perceptual positions: to see the world from customer/prospect's point of view when preparing for, and during, sales meetings.

- Resource anchor: to be in a useful state before and during the sales pitch, and possibly using words to anchor states in customers.

- Submodalities: to make sure your internal representations are as you would like them to be (remember the cold-calling example p.147).

- Hierarchy of Ideas: is it best to give the big picture or detail, or which combination?

- Reframing: to handle objections.

- Values: so that you can find out what the client/customer wants and demonstrate how your product or service meets their needs.

- Well-formed outcomes: for setting sales targets.

- Deep filters: to present information and to communicate in ways that suit the clients' filter preferences.

Recruitment

- Values elicitation: to find out what candidates want from a job or what employers are looking for, as well as finding out what the individual values mean.

- Deep filters: to match the preferences required for a role with those of the candidate.

Strategic planning

- Well-formed outcomes: to know where you want to be at given points in the future.

- Logical Levels: what is the corporate mission, corporate identity etc, and do these align with each other and the organisation's goals?

- Perceptual positions: to consider the organisation from the perspective of other stake-holders, and also from the perspective of a neutral market analyst/economic commentator.

Presentations

- Perceptual positions: to consider what the audience would want.

- Resource anchor: to ensure you feel good before and during the presentation.

- Anchoring states in the audience.

- Metaphors: stories and analogies often captivate audiences and can help you explain complex points.

- Reframing: especially if there are questions.

NLP AND COACHING

- Explaining to clients up-front about Cause and Effect, and the importance of taking full responsibility for their results. If clients accept this, your job as a coach is much easier than if they don't accept it.

- Having a good knowledge of the mindset for success is important. Often, the reason clients have challenges and have not achieved their goals is because in some way they are not adopting the mindset for success. For example, clients may actually believe they have failed, yet by taking it as feedback, their mindset will shift.

- Well-formed outcomes. The reasons why many clients benefit from NLP coaching is because it helps them be clear on their goals. Knowing what clients want is an essential starting point for coaching.

- All of the techniques mentioned in this book are useful, because if the client has a 'problem' you can use the relevant technique(s) to help them resolve it. Also with topics such as well-formed goals, rapport, some aspects of language, perceptual positions, values and deep filters, you can inform your clients of these so that they can use them as appropriate.

NLP AND SPORT

- Well-formed goals: so that you know what you want from your participation, as well as from each training session.

- Resource anchor: (including the visualisation of the future scenarios) to be in the right state, both before and during competition.

- Submodalities: to manage any negative self-talk.

- Perceptual positions: so that you can consider the tactics and game-plan from your opponent's point of view, as well as a neutral observer's.

- Reframing: turning disappointments and defeats into opportunities to improve.

NLP AND RELATIONSHIPS

- Perceptual position: to see other points of view (see conflict prevention and resolution in *NLP in the workplace* above).

- The Hierarchy of Ideas and chunking: many communication difficulties come from mis-matches of communication between *big picture* and *details*.

- Other deep filters: so that you can understand each other even better.

- Reframing: for example turning 'arguments' into 'opportunities to understand each other better'.

AND FINALLY...

NLP contains a series of techniques to help improve communication and change behaviours. When used wisely, carefully and ecologically, NLP can make a huge difference to people lives.

Please use these techniques only for the good of yourself and those around you. There are numerous NLP courses available, including those run by the author, most of which can help you develop and enhance your knowledge in a supervised environment. Appendix C gives some information regarding NLP courses available and what to consider when choosing one. References and further reading, and contact details, are provided after the appendices.

Thank you for reading *Successful NLP*. I sincerely hope you enjoyed it and found it beneficial to you. Do feel free to contact me (info@ thelazarus.com) if you have any questions, or to let me know how you have successfully used some of this material.

PART 5

APPENDICES

Appendix A: Preferred Representational System Questionnaire

STEP ONE: for each of the following statements, please place a score next to every phrase. Use the following system to rank your preferences:

4 = Most accurately describes your preference

3 = Next best description of your preference

2 = Next best description after 3 above of your preference

1 = Least likely description of your preference

At this point, ignore the reference to a, b, c and d. You will be using this information in step two. Please note that the order of a, b, c and d changes for each question.

1. **Generally I make important decisions based on:**
   a ＿＿ which way looks best to me
   b ＿＿ which way sounds the best to me
   c ＿＿ review, analysis and consideration of the issues
   d ＿＿ my gut level feelings, what feels best to me

2. **During a heated debate, I am most likely to be influenced by:**
   b ＿＿ people's tone of voice
   a ＿＿ whether or not I can see the other person's point of view
   c ＿＿ the logic of the other person's argument
   d ＿＿ how I feel about the topic(s)

3. **During a meeting, I like information to be presented:**

   a ____ in a way that is neat and tidy, with pictures and diagrams

   d ____ in a way that I can grasp and/or that I can get a hands-on experience

   c ____ in a logical, rational way, so that I can understand

   b ____ in the form of a conversation, so that we can discuss and I can ask questions

4. **My favourite hobbies and pastimes typically involve:**

   b ____ listening to music, the radio or talking with people

   a ____ watching films and other visual arts

   d ____ doing sport, activities and generally moving about

   c ____ reading, learning, analysing and generally using my mind

5. **I tend to resolve problems by:**

   a ____ looking at the situation and all the alternatives, possibly using diagrams

   b ____ talking through the situation with friends or colleagues

   c ____ analysing the situation and choosing the approach that makes most sense

   d ____ trusting my intuition and gut feelings

6. **When with my friends:**

   a ____ I enjoy watching how they interact and behave

   d ____ I tend to hug them, or sit close to them, when speaking to them

   c ____ I am interested in their rationale, reasons and ideas when talking to them

   b ____ I enjoy talking and listening to them

7. **I prefer to learn a particular aspect of a sport or activity by:**

   a ___ Watching how the teacher or coach does it

   d ___ Having the teacher or coach adjust my body into the right position

   b ___ Listening to explanations, discussing and asking questions

   c ___ Understanding the reasons and rationale for doing it in a certain way

8. **When at a presentation, I am most interested by:**

   c ___ The logic and a rationale of the presentation

   b ___ The tone of voice and way the presenter speaks

   a ___ The visual aids used by the presenter

   d ___ The opportunity to get to grips with the content, perhaps by actually doing an activity

Scoring the questionnaire

STEP TWO: transfer your scores from the above questions into the following table. For example, if your scores for question 8 are '1' for the first statement, '4' for the second statement, '3' for the third statement and '2' for the fourth statement, in row 8 you would put '1' in column 'c', '4' in column 'b', '3' in column 'a' and '2' in column 'd', as illustrated in this example:

8. **When at a presentation, I am most interested by:**

   c 1 The logic and a rationale of the presentation

   b 4 The tone of voice and way the presenter speaks

   a 3 The visual aids used by the presenter

   d 2 The opportunity to get to grips with the content, perhaps by actually doing an activity

	a	b	c	d
8	3	4	1	2

	a	b	c	d
1				
2				
3				
4				
5				
6				
7				
8				
TOTAL	Visual =	Auditory =	Auditory Digital =	Kinaesthetic =

STEP THREE: the totals give an indication of your relative preference for each of the four major Representational Systems (a = Visual, b = Auditory, c = Auditory Digital, d = Kinaesthetic). Remember, these scores are preferences, **not** statements about capability or about who you are as a person.

Appendix B: Summary of deep filters

Spectrum	Key traits	Summary of influencing approaches
Towards	Stays focused on goals and targets.	Mention what they would win, achieve, have, get, include, obtain. Give targets and target dates.
Away From	Notices what is wrong, or problems to be avoided/solved.	Mention situations to avoid, or things that we/they don't want to happen. Give deadlines.
Options	Seeks new and different ways to do things, willing to bend rules, dislikes following procedures.	Be flexible, offers several options.
Procedures	Likes to follows established procedures.	Offer/suggest the 'right' way to do something. Mention the steps or procedures to be taken.
Internal	Sets their own standards, knows what is right from their own judgements.	Use phrases such as 'you may want to consider', 'what do you think?', 'only you can decide'.
External	Needs feedback and input from others.	Mention what other people or other sources say or think.

Sameness	Likes things to stay the same, dislikes change, notices commonalities.	Keep things the same, or point out how the situation is similar to what they know.
Difference	Likes frequent and significant changes, notices how things are different.	Create frequent and major changes, point out how things have changed or are different.
Big picture	Thinks in overview and conceptually. Dislikes detail.	Provide overviews, and use words like 'essentially', 'overall', 'in summary'.
Detail	Likes and needs detail.	Provide details, and use words like 'precisely,' 'exactly', 'specifically'.

Appendix C: NLP Training

There are numerous NLP training courses available. Indeed there are so many that sometimes the choice can seem overwhelming. This appendix aims to clarify the situation for you. We will consider the types of training, the different levels within the 'hierarchy' of NLP qualification and a comment about standards.

BACKGROUND

It is important to be aware that there are different approaches to training NLP, and that at the time of writing there is no one set standard or governing body. There are several NLP 'Boards' and there are some significant variations within its membership in terms of:

- Style of delivery of training

- Approach to ethics and ecology

- Length of training required for certification

- Course syllabi

- The number of trainers required to certify students

Some of these variations will become apparent as you read on.

Training courses fall broadly into two types – certificated and non-certificated.

NON-CERTIFICATED COURSES

These range from half day seminars to courses lasting a few days. They tend to be introductions to NLP, possibly aimed at certain audiences (such as business, sales, managers, sports, and personal development). They may also deal with specific aspects of NLP such as improving communication. These courses may be taught by people who are not certified NLP Trainers as well as those who are Certified trainers.

CERTIFICATED COURSES

There are five levels of certifications. In order of hierarchy these are:

- Diploma
- Practitioner
- Master Practitioner
- Trainer
- Master Trainer

Neither Diploma nor Practitioner courses require any previous NLP experience, whereas the other three levels require delegates to be certified to the previous level.

NLP Diploma

Diploma courses last 30 hours, normally over four days, and the subjects taught are similar to the techniques covered in this book. These courses are useful for people who want to gain a solid grounding in improving communication and some of the aspects of changing behaviours. These courses are mainly aimed at people who want to use NLP for themselves as opposed to with others.

NLP Practitioner

There are two main types of Practitioner course:

- Those that last around 50 hours
- Those that last around 125 hours

The content of both types of course is broadly similar in that they cover most of the Diploma content, plus more of the techniques for changing behaviours and beliefs as well as further language skills.

I have heard delegates who have done both types say that the shorter courses generally provide an 'unconscious' capability, and that the longer courses generally provide both conscious and unconscious understanding and capability. Each potential student will need to decide for themselves what they require from their Practitioner training in terms of depth (and possibly breadth) and how they will want to use the material. Those wishing to use NLP with others, for example coaches, managers, trainers and business consultants, may well have different requirements than those primarily seeking the personal development aspects of NLP.

Within the category of training lasting 125 hours there are two main types:

- Face to face, lasting 15 to 20 days over several modules

- Approximately 50 to 60 hours of pre-course study plus 7 to 10 days of face to face training. The face to face training may be in one block or may be spread over modules, depending on the training organisation.

If students wish to undertake the 125 hours of training, then they would need to decide which of the two styles of training suits their learning style, their requirements from the training and the amount of time they have available.

Master Practitioner

Master Practitioner courses build on the content taught at Practitioner level (Practitioner certification is a pre-requisite for Master Practitioner courses) and cover new material regarding communication and language, changing behaviours and beliefs, as well as modelling. These courses usually provide deeper levels of personal development and broaden and deepen students' capability to facilitate 'change work' with other people.

Whilst the syllabus of Practitioner courses is relatively similar across the different NLP training, the content of Master Practitioner is more varied.

In terms of hours again there are different standards, the two main types of course being:

- Those that last around 65 hours, 9 days

- Those that last around 125 hours

The 125 hour style courses tend to be either:

- Face to face, lasting typically 16 to 20 days (normally modular)

- 14 days face to face (some courses are modular, some are *en bloc*) plus 30 to 40 hours of pre-course preparation

Similar considerations apply for choosing a Master Practitioner course as for choosing a Practitioner course.

It is important to note that Practitioners and Master Practitioners may run training courses and workshops, only Certified Trainers are able certify students as Practitioners or Master Practitioners.

NLP Trainer and Master Trainer

NLP Trainers have met the criteria of a Certified Trainers' Training which is open only to Master Practitioners. They are able to certify people at the level of Diploma, Practitioner and Master Practitioner. Trainers' Training courses will vary in terms of content and duration, ranging from 7 days to 19 days. Generally an effective NLP Trainers' Training course will:

- Teach students how to run NLP courses and how to teach and certify at NLP Diploma, Practitioner and Master Practitioner level

- Teach students excellent presentation skills

- Thoroughly test their knowledge of NLP

A typical and thorough evaluation process lasts four days.

Master Trainers have usually been Certified Trainers for several years and will be very experienced. Master Trainers can certify NLP Trainers and other Master Trainers.

Considerations when choosing a course

Whichever type of course you choose it is recommended that you satisfy yourself that the course will provide you with what you want from the course. Here are some considerations you may want to take into account:

- The reputation and qualifications of the trainer(s)

- The duration of the course

- The style of the course (such as modular or block, pre-course study or all face to face)

- The number of qualified assistants available to ask questions, observe and give feedback during exercises

- The body/board that recognises the course

- The pass rate (if everyone passes, what is the qualification worth?)

- The process and standards for certification

- The size of the training course (5, 50 or 500 delegates?)

- The follow-up support available

- The specialist subjects covered by the course (such as sport, business, personal development, health), and are they what you want?

- How many trainers are required to certify students

NLP is still a fairly new profession and has yet to establish a set of universally-recognised training criteria. This is reflected in the somewhat varied standards of training available, both in terms of assessment criteria and course content. One notable exception to this is NLP Psychotherapy training, which has set standards of training recognised by the UK Council for Psychotherapy.

Courses available from the author

The Lazarus Consultancy Ltd offers several NLP courses, for example:

- **Fast-Track Certified NLP Practitioner** (9 days plus pre-study, approximately 140 hours in total).

- **Fast-Track Certified NLP Master Practitioner** (14 days plus pre-study, approximately 140 hours in total).

- **Certified NLP Trainers' Training and Evaluation** (17 days plus pre-study).

- **Fast-Track Certified NLP Sports Practitioner** (2 days plus pre-study, for NLP Practitioners only).

- **Certified NLP Diploma, Sports Diploma and Business Diploma** (4 days, approximately 30 hours).

- **Introduction to NLP** courses, for business, coaching and sport (1 or 2 days).

Contact the author or visit www.thelazarus.com for further details and updated information.

References and further reading

Books

Deep Filters and Values
- Charvet, Shelle Rose, *Words That Change Minds: Mastering the Language of Influence* (Kendall/Hunt Publishing, 1995).

- Hall, L Michael and Bodenhamer, Bob, *Figuring Out People: Design Engineering With Meta-Programs* (Crown House Publishing, 1997).

General
- Covey, Stephen R, *The 7 Habits of Highly Effective People: Powerful Lessons in Personal Change* (Simon & Schuster, 1992).

Health and the Mind-Body Link
- Chopra, Deepak MD, *Quantum Healing: Exploring The Frontiers of Mind/Body Medicine* (Bantam Books, 1989).

- Leader, Darian, and Corfield, David, *Why Do People Get Ill? Exploring the Mind-body Connection* (Penguin Books, 2007).

Metaphors
- Rosen, Sidney, *My Voice Will Go With You: The Teaching Tales of Milton H. Erickson* (W W Norton & Co., 1982).

Meta-Model Language
- Bandler, Richard and Grinder, John, *The Structure of Magic, Volume I.* (Science and Behaviour Books Inc, 1975). Chapter 5 (p.69) is the relevant chapter.

Milton Model Language

- Bandler, Richard and Grinder, John, *Patterns of the Hypnotic Techniques of Milton H. Erickson, MD, Volume 1.* (Meta Publications, 1975).

- Bandler, Richard and Grinder, John, *Patterns of the Hypnotic Techniques of Milton H. Erickson, MD, Volume 2.* (Meta Publications, 1975).

- Moine, Donald and Lloyd, Kenneth, *Unlimited Selling Power: How to Master Hypnotic Selling Skills* (Prentice Hall, 1990). Also useful for Selling.

Modelling

- Dilts, Robert, *Modelling with NLP,* (Meta Publications, 1998).

NLP: Coaching

- O'Connor, Joseph and Lages, Andrea, *Coaching With NLP: A practical guide to getting the best out of yourself and others* (Element (HarperCollins), 2004).

NLP: General

- Bodenhamer, Bob and Hall, L Michael, *The User's Manual For The Brain Volume I and Volume II.* (Crown House Publishing, 1999 and 2003 respectively).

- Dilts, Robert and DeLozier, Judith, *Encyclopaedia of Neuro-Linguistic Programming and NLP New Coding* (NLP University Press, 2000).

- Ready, Romilla and Burton, Kate, *Neuro Linguistic Programming For Dummies* (John Wiley & Sons Ltd, 2004).

- O'Connor, Joseph, *NLP Workbook: a practical guide to achieving the results you want* (Element (HarperCollins), 2001).

NLP: Health

- Dilts, Robert, Hallbom, Tim and Smith, Suzi, *Beliefs – Pathways to Health & Well-Being* (Metamorphous Press, 1990).

NLP: Selling

- Johnson, Kerry L, *Selling with NLP* (Nicholas Brealey Publishing, 1994).

- O'Connor, Joseph and Prior, Robin, *Successful Selling With NLP: Powerful ways to help you connect with your customers* (Thorsons (HarperCollins), 1995).

NLP: Sport

- Lazarus, Jeremy, *Ahead of the Game: How to Use Your Mind to Win in Sport* (Ecademy Press, 2006).

- There are various e-books on the mental aspects of sport (based on NLP techniques) available on www.WinningAtSport.com, a website owned by the author dedicated to the uses of NLP in sport.

NLP: Therapy

- Bolstad, Richard, **Resolve: A New Model of Therapy** (Crown House Publishing, 2002).

- Wake, Lisa, *Neurolinguistic Psychotherapy: A Postmodern Perspective* (Routledge, 2008).

NLP: Work

- Knight, Sue, *NLP At Work: The Difference That Makes The Difference* (Nicholas Brealey Publishing, 1995).

Personality Traits (Myers Briggs Type Indicator)

- Keirsey, David and Bates, Marilyn, *Please Understand Me –*

Character & Temperament Types (Prometheus Nemesis Book Company Ltd, 1984).

Sport: Mental Aspects

- Hemery, David, *Sporting Excellence – What Makes A Champion?* (CollinsWillow, 1986).

- Grout, Jeff and Perrin, Sarah, *Mind Games – Inspirational Lessons From The World's Biggest Sports Stars* (Capstone (Wiley), 2004).

- Gallwey, W. Timothy, *The Inner Game Of Tennis* (Pan Books, 1974).

Submodalities

- Bandler, Richard, *Using Your Brain For A Change* (Real People Press, 1985).

- Andreas, Steve and Connirae, *Change Your Mind And Keep The Change* (Real People Press, 1987).

Also available from the author

- *The NLP Pocket Handbook*. An 80 page, A6 guide to the NLP Practitioner and Master Practitioner material. Available from www.thelazarus.com.

Audio material

There are several providers of NLP-related audio material ranging from one or two topics through to Practitioner and Master Practitioner level CD sets.

Available from the author

There are the following CDs available from The Lazarus Consultancy, covering most of the topics contained in this book.

- *NLP Practitioner CD Series:* A 16 CD set, lasting approximately 12½ hours, with a fully-referenced training manual. This comprises the pre-study material for The Lazarus Consultancy Fast-Track NLP Practitioner Course.

- *Understanding, Predicting and Influencing Behaviour – 4 CD Series:* A 4 CD set, lasting 4½ hours, covering the values and deep filters referred to in this book plus many more, with a fully-referenced manual.

- *Understanding, Predicting and Influencing Behaviour – 6 CD NLP Series:* The same as the 4 CD set above, plus two additional CDs covering how to change values and deep filters. For this reason this set is relevant only to NLP Practitioners and Master Practitioners.

Other audio material

The author will be developing further audio and DVD material, including interviews. These will be available on both www.thelazarus.com and www.WinningAtSport.com.

GLOSSARY

Anchor A representation/stimulus connected to and triggering a subsequent response. Anchors can be naturally occurring or set up deliberately.

Associated The memory of an experience as if seen through your own eyes.

Auditory Digital (Ad) The *Representational System* dealing with logic and the way we talk to ourselves.

Beliefs *Generalisations* we make about the world and our opinions about it. They form the rules about what we can and cannot do.

Calibration The ability to notice and measure changes with respect to a standard. Usually involves the comparison between two different sets of external, non-verbal cues.

Chunking Changing a perception by moving a 'chunk', or a group of bits of information, in the direction of more abstraction, more detail or laterally, through the use of language.

Content Reframe See *Meaning Reframe*.

Context The particular setting or situation in which the content occurs.

Context Reframing Giving another meaning to a statement by changing the context.

Cross-Over Matching *Matching* one aspect of a person's external behaviour or physiology with a different physiological movement.

Deep Filter See *Meta Programmes*

Deletion Deletion occurs when we leave out a portion of our experience as we make our *Internal Representations*.

Dissociated The memory of an experience, seeing your whole body in the picture.

Distortion Distortion occurs when something is mistaken for that which it is not, or when things that have not occurred are included in our *Internal Representations*.

Driver The *Submodality* that makes the most difference in our meaning of an experience.

Ecology The study of the consequences or results or impact of any change that occurs on the wider system.

First Position This is one of the *Perceptual Positions*. First Position is when you are seeing a situation from your own point of view.

Future Pace Mentally rehearsing a future result.

Generalisation Generalisation occurs when one specific experience represents or is generalised to a whole class of experiences.

Hierarchy of Ideas The level of abstraction of ideas and concepts, ranging from abstract to specific. The Hierarchy of Ideas can also be used for lateral thinking.

Internal Representations The content of our thinking or the confirmation of information which includes pictures, sounds, feelings, tastes, smells, and self talk.

Leading Changing your own behaviour with enough *Rapport* so another person will follow.

Logical Levels A model frequently used in NLP to classify our thinking and situations into the following categories: environment, behaviours, capabilities, beliefs and values, identity and purpose/mission. The model is sometimes known as 'Neurological Levels'.

Matching Replicating, to some degree, one or more aspects of a person's physiology or voice.

Meaning Reframe Giving another meaning to a statement by considering other (more positive) possible meanings. (Sometimes called a *Content Reframe*.)

Meta Model A model of language, derived from Virginia Satir that gives us an 'over' view of language. It allows us to recognise Deletions, Generalisations and Distortions in our language, and gives us questions to clarify imprecise language and gain specificity.

Meta Programmes These are unconscious, content-free programmes we run which filter our experiences (referred to as *Deep Filters* in this book).

Milton Model A set of language patterns used by Milton Erickson. These patterns use language in an abstract way, so that people can create their own meaning from Milton Model language used.

Mirroring Reflecting the physiology of someone as if looking into a mirror.

Modalities Refers to our *Internal Representations*, which relate to the five senses (*Visual, Auditory, Kinaesthetic, Olfactory, Gustatory*) plus our internal dialogue.

Modelling Modelling is the process by which all of NLP was created. In Modelling we elicit what someone does in their mind and physiologically that allows them to produce a certain behaviour. Then we codify these in a series of steps designed to make the behaviour easy to reproduce.

NLP Communication Model A model of how people internally process external events, and how this internal processing impacts on behaviours and results.

Pacing Gaining and maintaining *Rapport* with another person over a period of time by *Matching* or *Mirroring* their external behaviour and/or voice.

Perceptual Position Describes points of view in a specific situation: *First Position* is our own point of view. *Second Position* is usually someone else's point of view. *Third Position* is the point of view of a dissociated observer – much like an overview.

Predicates Words and phrases that often presuppose one of the *Representational Systems.*

Preferred Representational System This is the *Representational System* that someone most often uses to think, to organise his or her experiences, and that we commonly and most easily employ.

Presuppositions of NLP Assumptions or convenient beliefs, which are not necessarily 'true', but which if accepted and believed will change our thinking and improve our results.

Principles for Success These are six principles which, when adhered to increase our chances of success, both for individual tasks and in life generally. The six principles are: know your outcome; use sensory acuity to take feedback; be flexible; build and maintain *Rapport*; operate from a physiology and psychology of excellence; take action.

Rapport The ability to relate to others in a way that creates a climate of trust and understanding.

Reframing The process of making a shift in the nature of a problem or changing the structure or context of a statement to give it another meaning.

Representational System This is the way we code sensory information and experience our world. There is a Representational System for each of our senses.

Resources Resources are the means to create change within oneself or to accomplish an outcome. Resources may include certain *States* or adopting specific physiology.

Resourceful State This refers to any *State* where a person has positive, helpful emotions available to him or her, and is operating from them behaviourally.

Second Position Relating to a *Perceptual Position*. Second Position is the point of view of the other person(s) involved in the situation.

Sensory Acuity The ability to notice and gain awareness of another person's conscious and unconscious responses through their physiology and/or voice.

State Our internal emotional condition.

Submodalities These are fine distinctions (or the subsets of the *Modalities*) that are part of each *Representational System* that encode and give meaning to our experiences.

Third Position Relating to a *Perceptual Positions*. Third Position is the point of view of a dissociated observer, an overview.

Values Criteria which are important to you, what you look for or want in something.

Well-Formed Conditions The Well-Formed Conditions allow us to specify goals and outcomes that are more achievable, because the way the goal is set conforms to certain rules/principles.

Well-Formed Outcomes These are goals and outcomes which are stated and set in a way that meets the *Well-Formed Conditions*.